ISLANDS OF THE VENETIAN LAGOON
AERIAL GUIDE

Project and Photography   Arturo Colamussi

Maps   Diego Tiozzo Netti

Flights   AERNOVA s.r.l.

Editor

ENDEAVOUR

D1107266

Table of contents

On the cover:
L'Ottagono Abbandonato

Editor

ENDEAVOUR

Endeavour Ricerca e Sviluppo
Via Cortile 1
44100 Ferrara

Project and photos   Arturo Colamussi

Maps   Diego Tiozzo Netti

Flights   Aernova s.r.l. Forlì

Print   Litografia Tosi - Ferrara
April 2007
October 2007

ISBN   97888-89922-03-3

Copyright   Endeavour
Ricerca e Sviluppo

This guide structure is protected by a patent application (pending).

6.

Over the Lagoon

I've often had to fly over the Lagoon for my job.

It was only after publishing a book on the Po River Delta and then a second one on the region of Molise, though, that we accepted the challenge of publishing yet a third on the Lagoon. Perhaps rather rashly so this time, given the notoriety of the place and the abundance of literature on the subject!

But there are strong points to recommend the enterprise. First, there are aerial views. And then there's a new underlying idea as to what a guidebook should be, and namely a perfect balance of pictures and text with clear indications to the reader as to the geographical location of the places illustrated.

So, off we went to Forlì to knock once again on the door of the Aeronova Air Work Company. Fortunately, its manager, Giancarlo Giunchi, is a long-time friend who shares my passion for photography.

A lot of flights were arranged in Summer and Autumn. Photographer and pilot shared the same emotions, ranging from veritable joy to gloom at the pitiful conditions - all the more conspicuous from above – of many of the Lagoon's islands

As with our previous Guides, we surfed the web for much of the minimal information accompanying the shots.

Our "e-references" are acknowledged in the book along with other sites contacted, whose information, though, we haven't used directly.

Maps were provided by Diego Tiozzo Netti. His website, MILVa (Interactive Map of the Venice Lagoon), triggered our meeting.

The layout follows an ideal South to North route with several turn-offs, more than anything for reasons dependant on the artwork.

Working on the Guide brought me in touch with a number of agencies whose work, of the sort endorsed in the foreword, I had occasion to appreciate.

One of these agencies - not the only one of course - was the Venice Lagoon Forum. Spurred on by its C.E., Guglielmo Russo, the Forum is actively engaged in carrying forward a sustainable development and a fight-against-poverty project, the latter with special reference to the Mediterranean and the Black Sea, which I believe deserves our wholehearted attention and backing.

I wish to thank here the Forum for its contribution in providing information on the minor islands of the Lagoon.

Arturo Colamussi
arturo.colamussi@tin.it

Chioggia

Chioggia had certainly already been established during Roman times. Fugitives from the mainland following on the invasions of the Huns and the Longobards in 452 and 568, respectively led to an increase in the Island's population.

Chioggia was sacked and looted twice, and namely by Pippin the Short, King of the Franks in 810, and by the Magyars in 902.

In 1110 it was designated as an episcopal see and the relics of its Patron Sts. Felix and Fortunatus were taken over from Malamocco where they had in turn been brought from Aquileia. Clugia Major (Chioggia) and Clugia Minor (Sottomarina) were subsequently placed under the dominion of the Venetian Republic and subject to the authority of its Chief Magistrate, the Doge. Between 1379 and 1380 Chioggia was the scene of a famous war between the Maritime Republics of Genoa and Venice which takes its name from the city.

After having razed to the ground Sottomarina, which was to be rebuilt only in 1700, the Genoese besieged Chioggia. The siege was subsequently lifted by the Venetian fleet.

In 1797 following on the fall of the Venetian Republic, Chioggia was occupied by the French. In 1798 the treaty of Campoformio assigned the city to the Austrians. The people of Chioggia opposed their dominion and attempted to shake it off in a famous rebellion known as the "Sollevazione del Cristo" on 20 April 1800.

French and Austrian domination continued alternatively for the next fifty years or so. Chioggia's role in the Italian Risorgimento was very important, so much so that it was in fact awarded a gold medal thanks to the participation of seventy of its citizens in Garibaldi's campaign for Italian unity. Chioggia was annexed to the Kingdom of Italy on 15 October 1866. The effects of World War I on Chioggia were extremely harsh. Following Italian retreat and establishment of the front line on the River Piave, Chioggia in fact became the immediate rearguard and many civic and ecclesiastical buildings were converted into military hospitals.

Chioggia once again played a strategic military role during the closing stages of World War II. The allies in fact were considering the possibility of a landing at Chioggia with the support of local freedom fighters so as to occupy the coastline fortifications and hence gain military control of the Veneto as a whole.

.9

Cà Roman

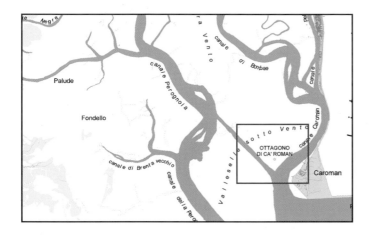

Under threat from the Turks and following the recommendations of a special committee appointed for the purpose, towards the end of the fifteenth century the Venetian Senate ordered the construction of a number of octagonal forts to defend the harbour-mouths. Provisional stone-, wood-, pile- and earth-works were probably already extant at the chosen sites.

The Cà Roman Octagon defended the port of Chioggia, while the Alberoni Octagon along with Forts Campana and Poveglia formed a line of defence against incursions by enemy vessels, effectively cutting off entry into the Malamocco Channel.
Following on the War of Candia, the Alberoni Octagon was further fortified in 1646.
After a long period of neglect, between 1726 and 1790 the Octagons were given a new lease of life following on changes in the extent of the Venetian Republic's dominions and the threat posed by the Hapsburgs.

In early 1800 the Octagons were included in an integrated defence system by the French under their command.

During the second period of Austrian domination, the artillery units of the Octagons were upgraded as part of a general strengthening of the defences on the Lagoon. Galleries were dug in the outer rampart walls, earthworks to a new design were thrown up, new casemates erected, and additional batteries put in.
Contemporary records show guns to have been placed on three of the eight sides, namely those facing the channel from where an assault was most likely to come. The three sides were further protected by massive bastions while those on the other five sides were not as high and thick.

The Cà Roman Octagon continued to be used by the military well into the twentieth century. The foundations of two structures, probably a watchtower and a bunker are still visible. A circular, gun-bearing cement platform probably dating to World War II may still be seen standing in the centre.

The Island is now deserted and overrun by vegetation.

Cà Roman bunkers

Pellestrina

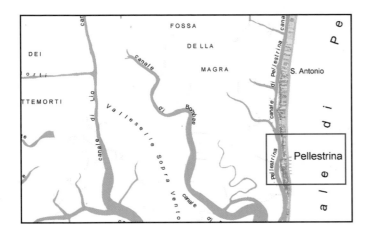

After being overrun and pillaged during the War of Chioggia in the fourteenth century, the Island was given a new lease of life by four noble families who settled on it. The Island was divided up into four districts along Venetian lines ("sestieri"), each named after one of the resident families.

The heavy floods of 1966 caused severe damage and destruction despite the colossal embankments designed by Vincenzo Coronelli in 1716 and erected under the direction of B. Zendrini in 1744 to protect the coastal towns and villages and the settlements in the Lagoon.

The Church of St. Mary of St. Vito stands on the site of an apparition of the Virgin. The current polygon-shaped church was built in 1723 to the design of the architect A. Tirali.

The Battle of Petervaradino was fought on 5 August 1716, the day after an unknown Lady appeared to a fourteen-year-old boy telling him

to have Masses said for the dead "if we are to have victory". The circumstance is astounding! The Fort of Petervarandino was the key for winning back Belgrade and recovering this area of the Balkans to the West.

"Vien qua fio
va' dal Piovan
e dighe
che faccia celebrar
delle messe
per le anime
del Purgatorio,
se volemo aver vittoria,
e portime la risposta;
e tel digo a ti
perchè ti xe degno".

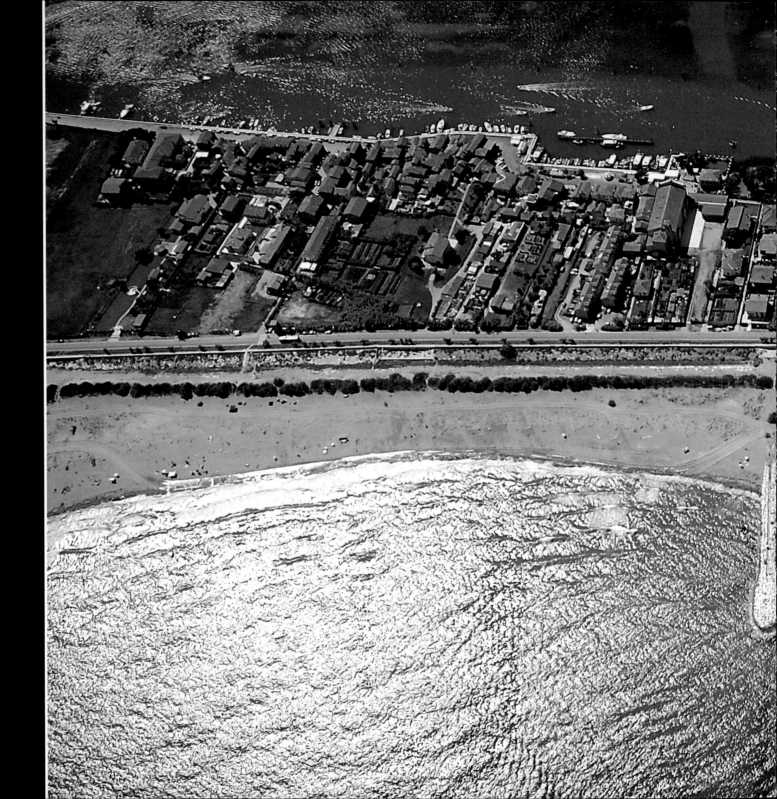

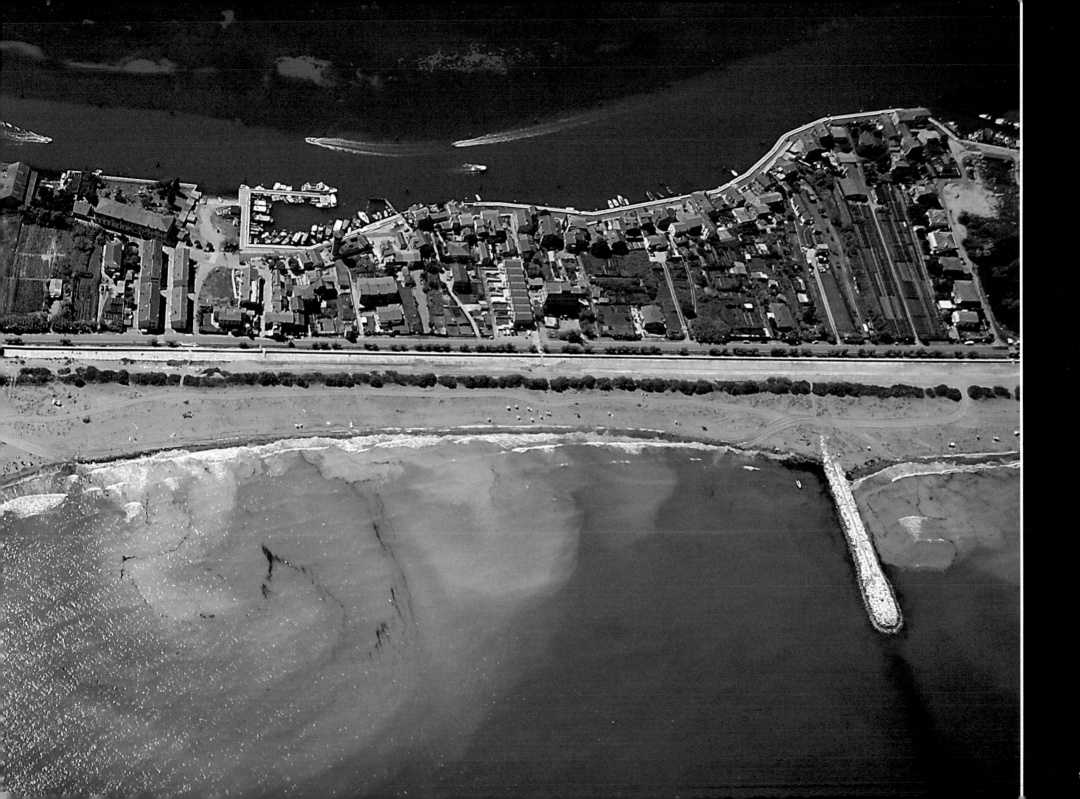

.19

Ottagono San Pietro

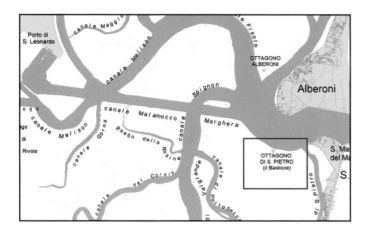

St. Peter's Octagon was the last line of fire against enemy ships managing to force the blockade of the forts around the Mouth of Malamocco.

After the War of Candia new and stronger defences were put in at the Octagon of St. Peter in 1646.

Throughout the first half of the twentieth century the Island was occupied by the military, being finally and completely evacuated in the sixties and seventies. It is now deserted and rather desolate. Its buildings are practically derelict. The ruins of possibly a guardhouse and of a mooring-landing situated on the protected side of the chief navigable canal are still visible.

Casone Valle Zappa

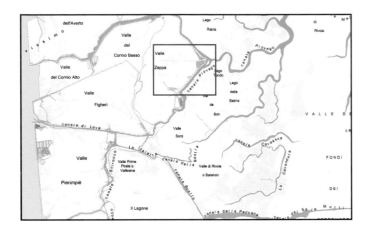

Built between 1925 and 1927 for the then owner, Mario Malvezzi, to a design by the architect Duilio Tores, no one can now say whether this Folly owes its bizarre style to the architects inventiveness or to his client's desire to "transplant a Dutch gem in the Lagoon".

To some extent the Valle Zappa casone may appear foreign as it has nothing in common with the other constructions of its kind. But it in fact perfectly fits into its context, adding yet a further touch of glamour to the watery landscape.
Aside from its unusual architecture, another peculiarity worth mentioning is the different colours in which each room is painted.

Guests arriving on Saturday evening were assigned a room by the master of the hunt according to the colour of the barrel they would be shooting from on the Sunday.

Malamocco harbour

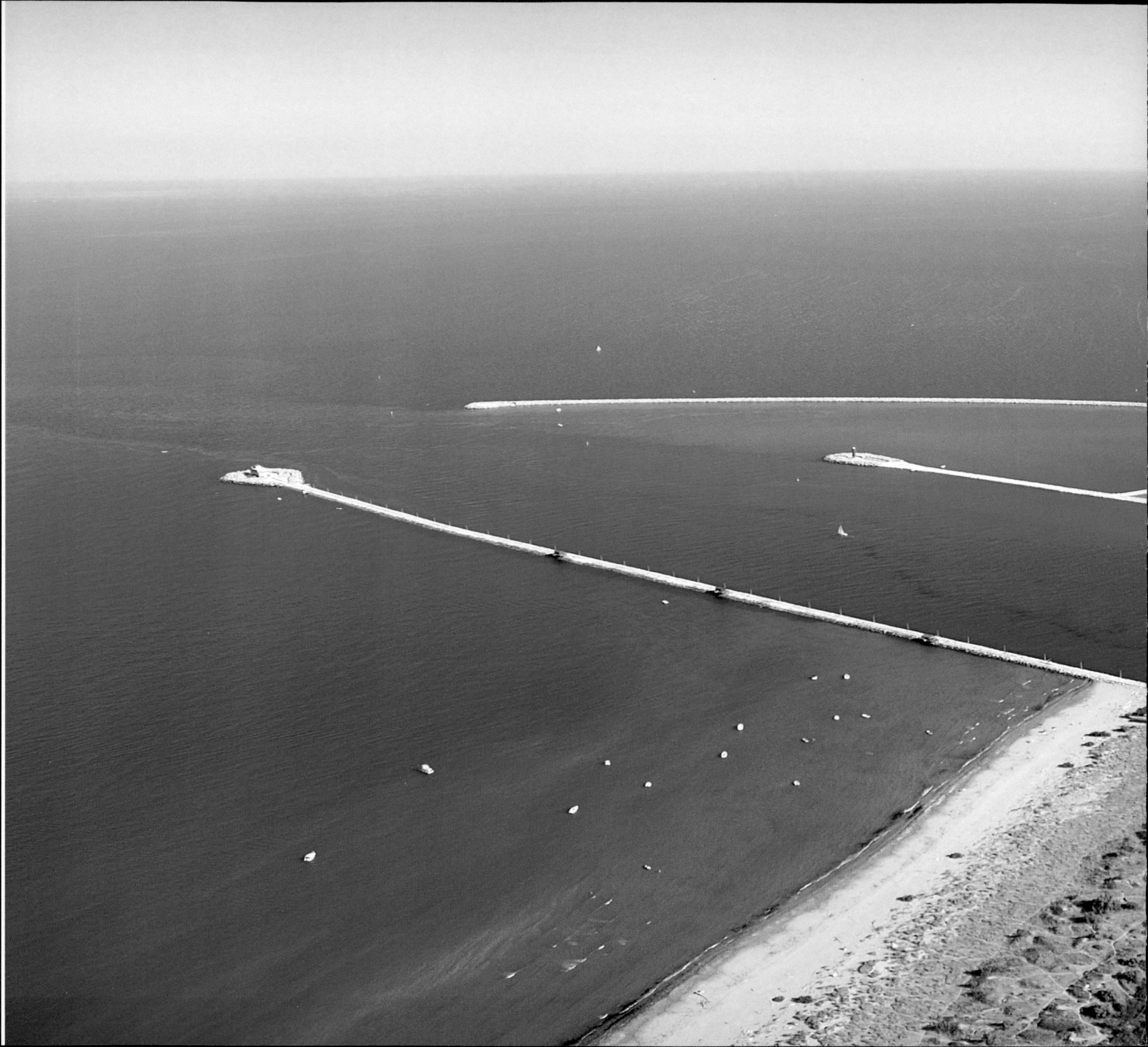

Alberoni

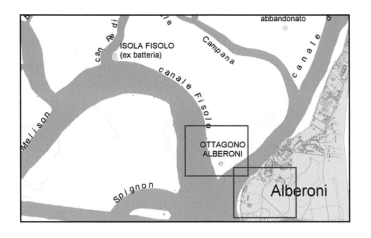

The first nine holes of the Venice Golf Club designed by the Scottish architect Cruickshank were opened in 1930.

The story has it that Henry Ford, the great automobile manufacturer then famous for his model "T", the first car to be mass produced, was a frequent visitor to Venice. On one occasion he inquired with Count Giuseppe Volpi of Misurata, President of the Italian Grand Hotel Company, where he might go for a game of golf. He was of course told that there were no links in Venice, but it was then that Count Volpi decided the time had come for there to be some, and indeed for the following year.

An area of only sand dunes was identified around Fort Alberoni and veritable Scottish style links were put in.

In 1951 the course was upgraded to eighteen holes.

Through the years it has been constantly improved on, without though betraying the original idea.

Famous players have golfed here. The record of sixty-seven strokes, five below par, is held by Arnold Palmer. Other champions include Henry Cotton, Johnny Miller, Severiano Ballesteros, Tony Jacklin, Lee Trevino, and many more.

The underlying sand base has been retained as in the original links, while additional undulating greens and ponds have been put in.

These along with Fort Alberoni are the challenging obstacles to be overcome at many a hole. Indeed, Fort Alberoni with its irregular star shape built by the Venetians in defence of the Lagoon is still today the most outstanding feature brooding over many a hole.

Number nine, for instance, with its three par blind is legendary. The player is confronted with the Fort's ditch and ramparts. Such a hole anywhere else would be absurd. Here it has achieved legendary status as the world-famous "number nine of Venice", appearing in many periodicals in Europe and overseas for the ingenious systems that have been installed to warn the player about to strike whether there's anyone else on the green.

Then there's hole eleven; a panel of experts have classified it as the best five par in Italy. But many of the others equally require faultless precision. The price paid for any error is high and the golfer's recovery skills are often put to the test.

Alberoni Octagon

Fisolo and Poveglia Batteries

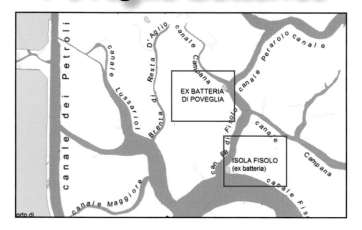

The Islands of Fisolo and of the former Battery Poveglia were part of a chain of artillery defences strung out along the Lagoon between Venice and the mainland at Mestre.

The batteries were originally erected on platforms resting on pile-works sunk deep into the sandbanks beneath the shallow waters and close to channel intersections.

In a letter dated 1797 and signed by Zuanne Zusto, a nobleman and official in charge of the surveillance and upkeep of the Lagoon and beaches, reference is made to works of the previous year, from which it appears that seven wooden forts for the defence of Venice had already been built.

As witnessed to by other documents dated 1883, all the artillery emplacements in the Lagoon were in earth with ramparts, magazines and small barracks.

Records of the Austrian High Command in Vienna report two types of earthwork batteries only slightly different in size but of the same shape with seven short sides almost forming a semi-circle and a long side.
Of the two types of batteries of different size mentioned in this document, that of Fisolo was the largest.

Today little is left of Fisolo except the clearly marked out ground plan, some of the higher enclosing rampart, and a few ruins, including pedestals and paving. The embankment had a twofold function, that of defending and camouflaging the platforms on which the guns were placed. The remains of the original artificial reef made up of blocks of even very large size may still be seen on the dry bank.

The "Venezia Nuova" Consortium has carried out works to rebuild the shoulders, banks and embankments, filling in with demolition material and landscaping the Island.

The somewhat peculiar comb-like configuration of the ex-Batteria Poveglia embankment and the masonry wall are probably ascribable to the need to adapt the battery to house anti-aircraft guns during World War I.
On the northern side of the Island the 260cm-high wall has collapsed. Because of erosion on the base of the longer side the wall stability is extremely precarious.
Two prism-shaped blocks emerging from the water near the shorter southern side are what's left of a jetty.

Fisolo island

Poveglia Battery

Poveglia island

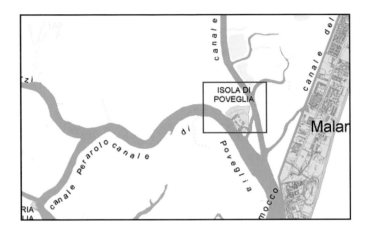

In the early fifth century the Island was a safe haven for the people of Padova and Este fleeing from the barbarian invasions.

Following on Pippin's invasion in 809 the inhabitants fled to the safety of the Rialto Islets.

In 864 to appease the retainers of the slain Chief Magistrate, Doge Pietro Tradonico, Doge Orso Partecipazio granted them the right to settle on the Island along with many other privileges. Over the following centuries the Island prospered both economically and population-wise; so much so that it was first governed by a Tribune, then by a Chamberlain appointed by the Doge and finally by a Podesta.

The octagonal fort on the Island was built to defend it during the war with Chioggia and the Island's inhabitants were moved for safety to the Giudecca.

Following on the war with Chioggia the Island was abandoned and the buildings left derelict. In view of these conditions the governing official (Magistrato alle Ragioni Vecchie) offered the Island to the monks of Camaldoli for them to build a convent but the offer was turned down.

In 1661 the native inhabitants were offered the buildings for reconstruction but also this offer was rejected.
Towards the end of the eighteenth century Poveglia passed under the jurisdiction of the sanitary authorities (Magistrato alla Sanità) and was used as a sanitary check-point for ship crews in transit and as a temporary goods store.
The Island was turned into a temporary lazaretto in 1793 following on a plague which had struck the crews of two ships.

In the early nineteenth century the Island was definitely converted to use as a lazaretto. Pursuant to a Napoleonic decree the church dedicated to St. Vitalis was demolished and the adjacent bell-tower set to use as a light-house.

A century later the Island was fitted out as a maritime station for the placing in quarantine of crews and passengers coming from ports where an epidemic had been reported. The sanitary complex was subsequently turned into a convalescent home for the aged.

In 1997 a project was drawn up for the Island by the Youth and Students Tourist Centre (CTS). The project envisaged the construction of a youth hostel and other facilities for cultural purposes. The Treasury Department withheld Poveglia from the saleable properties' list and reassigned it to the Lands Office for granting to CTS. In view of project implementation Island shoulders will have to be restored by the "Venezia Nuova" Consortium.

Santo Spirito

Records dated 1140 mention the presence of a hospital, a church and a convent of the Augustine Fathers on the Island.

In 1380 the Island was associated with the Brondolo Abbey and was granted by the Senate to the Cistercian Fathers of the Brondolo Trinity.

The Hermits of St. Augustine occupied the Island in 1430 and had the church rebuilt to a design by Sansovino. The church houses works by Titian, Bonifacio and Palma the Elder.

Following on the suppression of the Order of the Hermits of St. Augustine by Pope Alexander VII in 1656 the property of the Order was sold off and the works of art on the Island were moved to the Church of the Salute in Venice, at the time under construction. Friars Minor Observant fleeing from the Island of Candia settled on Santo Spirito in 1672.

In the early nineteenth century the Island was turned over to the French Government which assigned it to the War Fleet.

The Island's set-up was completely altered and part of the buildings were demolished to make room for military facilities.

Even though greatly changed, only the church and part of the convent are still extant.

The military stores were used throughout World War I, after which the Island was completely evacuated.
The gunpowder store already recorded in Coronelli's map of the islands is also mentioned in the 1932 land register; today the building is no longer extant.

Today the Island is completely deserted and the buildings have been gutted and vandalised.

Sacca Sessola

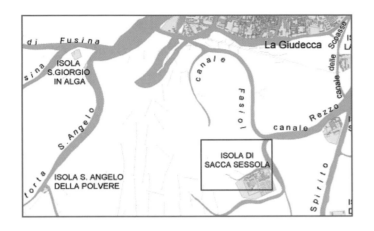

This artificial island was made between 1860 and 1870 using material dredged from the Maritime Station canals.

The Island was initially the property of the Royal Household before being transferred to the Municipality of Venice by a deed dated 2 July 1875. Facilities were erected on the area for use as a general petroleum depot. This utilization was discontinued in 1892.

A project was undertaken to build a hospital on Sacca Sessola for contagious endemic diseases.

In 1904 several stores were renovated and converted to hospital use. After the end of the cholera epidemic in 1911 it was decided to use the hospital for patients with other diseases. In 1914 the Hospital of St. Mark was opened for the long-term cure of pulmonary tuberculosis and patients who till then had been at the hospital on Grazia Island were moved here. The Sanatorium remained closed throughout World War I and only reopened in 1920.

The Romanesque-revival church was built in 1921 and the recreation pavilion in 1923. In 1927 the Venice City Council donated the Island to a State Agency (the future National Social Insurance Institute, INPS) for it to build a new 300-bed hospital.

Works were soon begun for the construction of a building with symmetrical wings intended to house the new facility. In 1936 the De Giovanni Hospital for Pulmonary Diseases, which for the time was extremely modern, was inaugurated by King Victor Emmanuel III.

The pavilions were set in extensive parklands, and the complex was equipped with all necessary facilities and amenities, including a motion-picture theatre and a water tower. Staff accommodation facilities were built in 1942 and required the demolition of the wards still in use of the old hospital.

In 1979 the Hospital was closed down and decay slowly set in.

The Island was turned over to the City Council with the proviso that it be used for the needs of the local Health Board.

In 1992 the Venice City Council placed the Island in the care of the Venice International Centre for Marine Sciences and Technologies.

Lazzaretto Vecchio

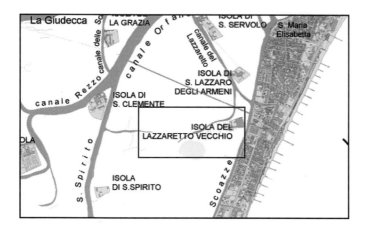

The Island was originally inhabited by the Hermits of St. Augustine who built a Church dedicated to St. Mary of Nazareth and a hospice for pilgrims travelling to and returning from the Holy Land.

In 1423 following the advice of St. Bernardine of Siena the authorities decided to use the Island for placing individuals and goods coming from infected countries.

The Lazaretto already occupied two islands linked by a bridge. A gunpowder store ("casello") and living quarters for the guards were hosted on the smaller.

The Lazaretto itself, which had incorporated the pre-existing monastic complex with the addition of wooden huts and sheds later replaced with buildings in masonry, was on the larger one.

It is believed that the term "Lazaretto" derives from "Nazaretum" (St. Mary of Nazareth), while the qualifier "Old" was meant to distinguish it from the "New" Lazaretto built in 1468.

In 1564 part of the adjacent lagoon was filled in to increase the Island's surface area .

Building of the mooring on the inlet side of the complex and other works of various extent and importance were carried out over the following three centuries.

The Island was subsequently taken over by the military authorities. Two sides of the cloister, the Church, the reception hall and other out buildings were demolished.

The bell-tower was demolished at the end of the nineteenth century.

In 1965 the military garrison finally evacuated the Island.

In the nineties the Lazaretto was assigned to a canine protection society for use as an asylum for stray dogs.

San Clemente

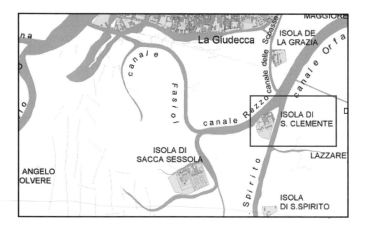

In 1288 the relics of St. Anian were laid to rest in St. Clement. The hospice was gradually converted into a monastery. Over the fourteenth century the Island lost its importance and gradually declined as rich donations diminished.

In 1432 the Venetian Gabriele Condulmer was elected Pope. The new Pope decided to move the Lateran Canons into St. Clement, which in the meantime had become practically deserted.

The new incumbents made alterations to the existing monastery and added on a double colonnaded cloister. The original Church also underwent radical renovation. The façade was completely done anew by the Lombardo family. Some older parts of the temple, however, survive to this day.

During the sixteenth century St. Clement was often used by the Republic to host visiting foreign monarchs and ambassadors but also as an asylum and health resort for patricians affected by contagious illnesses. During the plague of 1630 the Island was temporarily used as a lazaretto. At the end of the plague a Chapel modelled on the Holy House at Loreto was erected near the main altar to keep a vow, thus considerably altering the design of the Church.

In 1645 the Island was purchased by the monks of Camaldoli who set about restoring the Church and Convent and building an array of small dwellings, each with its annexed vegetable patch. In 1680 the Island was enlarged and surrounded by a wall; a new library was also built. Sometime during the seventeenth century the Church façade was restored and several side Chapels were built. A number of renowned artists were called in for these works, including Longhena and Giusto le Court.

After the fall of the Republic in 1797 the monks of Camaldoli abandoned the Convent and Church and the Island became the property of the State. The buildings were used by the Austrians for military purposes.

Owing to indiscriminate overcrowding at St. Servolo, in 1855 the Austrian Government decided to establish the Central Women's Mental Asylum of the Venetian Provinces on the Island of St. Clement. Three years later all pre-existing buildings on the Island except the Church were demolished. Rebuilding was begun in 1858 and lasted till 1873.

In 1859 the fortified tower built in 1500 for storing gunpowder crumpled.

Sant'Angelo della Polvere

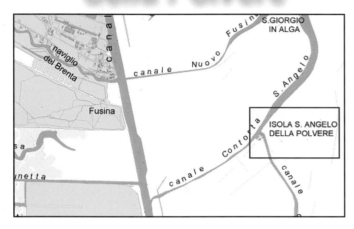

The Island was originally called Sant'Angelo di Concordia (St. Angel of Concord) from whence it was corrupted by the Venetians to Contorta.

Under the Doge (Chief Magistrate) Domenico Contarini a Benedictine church and monastery were built on the island in 1060. The Benedictine monks were subsequently replaced by nuns who dedicated the Convent to St. Michael Archangel. In 1474 these latter nuns were recalled to Venice for their bad conduct.

In 1518 the Island was placed in the care and custody of the Carmelite Fathers with the proviso that they restore the buildings.
A year after the departure of the friars in 1554 and after the fire at the Arsenal, the Senate decided to use the Island as a gunpowder factory. Two special covered barges ("burchielli") were built at the Arsenal for the transportation of explosives.

The buildings were struck by lightening in 1689 and almost razed to the ground along with the enclosing wall by the ensuing fire. After this calamity the Island was deserted for many decades.
A drawing dating to the eighteenth century shows the presence of a Venetian military installation on the Island. Wordings next to the buildings portrayed in the drawing read: "barracks", "magazine", "guardhouse". The garrison was enclosed by bastions. The same ground-plan is reported in a French lands office document. The French probably kept the complex erected by the Lagoon master builders unaltered until 1814.

After the Veneto's annexation to the Kingdom of Italy towards the end of the nineteenth century, the forts strung out across the Lagoon for defence were given a new lease of life. Fort Sant'Angelo as it appears today with its two large hangars and dividing earthen embankments probably dates back to this period. Oddly enough an Austrian map dated 1900 (Kriegsarkiv Vienna) shows the pre-1814 works still standing. The map may have been made with a view of the Hapsburgs taking back their former possessions but omits the changes that had occurred in the meantime and even mixes in several elements.

By mid twentieth century several new concrete structures were erected in the post World War II years, including the perimeter wall, the piezometer tower, the landing. The Fort was still under military command.

The Island is presently deserted and the buildings derelict.

.41

La Grazia

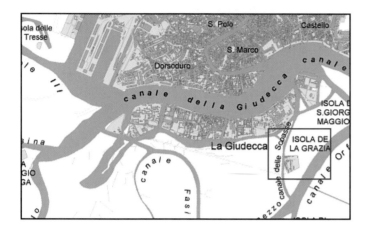

In the late tenth century Tribuno Memmo, the Venetian Chief Magistrate ("Doge"), granted the Monks of St. George a stretch of sandbar called the "Cavanella".

In 1264 progressive dumping of rubble on the sandbar gradually built up into an island on which a hospice for pilgrims to the Holy Land under the Cà di Dio (The House of God) was erected.

In 1412 the monks of St. George turned over the Island to the Congregation of St. Jerome of Fiesole.

The Congregation converted the hospice into a convent in 1439 and also built a church in which a painting of St. Mary of the Graces coming from Constantinople was placed, hence giving the island its name.

The church and convent were destroyed by a fire in 1528 but quickly rebuilt.

The Congregation of St. Jerome of Fiesole was suppressed by Pope Clement IX in 1668 and its property transferred to the Republic of Venice engaged in the War of Candia against the Turks.

In 1671 the till-then-deserted Island was purchased by Maria Felice Spinelli, a Capuchin nun of St. Jerome, for the purpose of settling here with other nuns of her order. With the aid of a number of devotees, the nuns set about having a church built dedicated to St. Mary of the Angels. This may rightly be considered the Island's heyday. The church was adorned by the works of famous painters including Tintoretto, Veronese and Longhi.

Pursuant to a Napoleonic decree the complex was suppressed in 1810 and the Island put to use as a powder magazine.

Two explosions in 1849 completely devastated the Island, destroying all traces of the monumental buildings.

Several pavilions given over to the cure of tuberculosis were built in the early twentieth century, their use being subsequently put to hosting patients suffering from other contagious diseases.

In 1952 a modernly equipped ward for poliomyelitic patients was opened.

The Island is today in a fairly good condition and the buildings in a fairly good state of repair.

San Giorgio in Alga

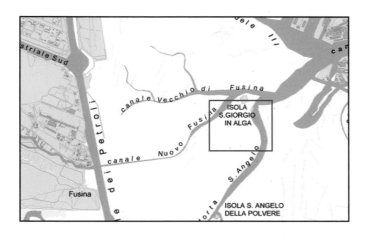

The first Benedictine monastery was established here sometime in the eleventh century.

In 1144 the church was consecrated and dedicated to St. George.

By 1216 the Island had acquired considerable status, so much so that it hosted the Chief Magistrate, Doge Pietro Ziani and the Patriarch of Aquileia.

Augustine monks replaced the Benedictine in 1350. The new occupants remained till the end of the fourteenth century when Pope Boniface IX erected the convent into a commendam, assigning the benefice to a Venetian patrician, Ludovico Barbo. The new incumbent brought in two young patricians who established the Congregation of Canons Secular.

By 1438 many buildings had fallen into ruin and the church and monastery had to be rebuilt. The monastery was completed in 1443, the bell-tower in 1454, and the church in 1458.

In 1668 the Order of the Canons Regular was suppressed by Pope Clement IX. The Island was next entrusted to the monks of St. Francis of Paola and then to the Barefooted Carmelites, who in 1690 and again 1716 carried out extensive restoration works.

The convent and richly endowed library were practically razed to the ground by a fire in 1717. The church was subsequently rebuilt by an unknown architect, possibly Andrea Tirali.

In 1799 the complex was used to detain political prisoners. The Island subsequently became the chief stronghold in the Austrian line of fortified defences inside the Lagoon.

In 1806 the monks withdrew to the Scalzi Monastery; the church was demolished and part of the convent reconverted for use as a powder-magazine.

The Island's military vassalage was to last for the rest of the nineteenth and up to the mid twentieth century. The Island was bombed in 1945 during the Second World War.

The anti-aircraft gun emplacements mounted for the Island's defence during World War II are still visible. Pillage and vandalism have been and continue to be the sad lot of the buildings.

.45

San Lazzaro degli Armeni

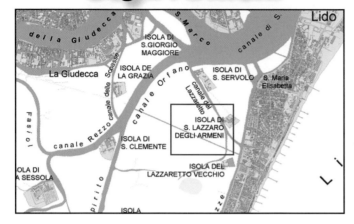

In 1185 the Island was donated by Hubert, the Abbot of St. Hilary, to Leone Parlini who established a church and monastery dedicated to St. Leo, Pope, along with a hospital for lepers.

By 1479 the Island's name, St. Lazarus, which comes from the time when the only inmates of the hospital were lepers, was consolidated .

By late fifteenth century following on a decline in the number of lepers, the establishment was slowly abandoned and in the end the Island was deserted for two centuries.

In 1717 the Senate permanently donated the Island to the Congregation of Mechitarist Armenian monks. The Church and Convent were rebuilt to the design of the Abbot Mechitar; the works lasted thirty years.
An important printing shop endowed with the characters of almost all Oriental languages was set up in 1789.

In the early nineteenth century Napoleon's ban of religious orders spared the Convent of the Mechitarist Armenian Fathers as it was considered a literary academia.

Land reclamation works were carried out on the north side of the Island in 1815.

The Island as it now appears is the result of further reclamation works carried out in 1912 and 1947.

The Church of St. Lazarus of the Armenians hosts a library of about 200,000 volumes and a museum with over 4,000 ancient Armenian manuscripts and a rich collection of Arab, Indian and Egyptian artefacts acquired by the monks or received as donations. Among the latter there is the unusual mummy of Nehmeket dating to 1000 B.C..

The monks conduct guided tours in a variety of languages.
The Island boasts a long tradition of hospitality for scholars and students of Armenia.

One of these was Lord Byron who studied Armenian here in 1816. A permanent exhibition recalls the event. The famous poet seems to have been especially partial to the rose petal jam called Vartanush.

The monks still produce it using petals from roses grown on the Island, some varieties of which very rare.

Campana island

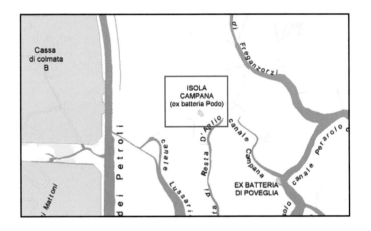

Campana Island is situated in the southern part of the Lagoon at the end of the Bell Canal, a few hundred metres from the Petroleum Canal. Its surface area is a little over 0.4 hectares.

The Islet is in fact artificial and was built in the last century as an artillery emplacement. It was evacuated at the end of the Second World War.

The Islet is today in a rather neglected state.

Excursionists occasionally land here and use it to cook their picnics or for a bit of sunbathing.

Flotsam and carelessly dumped rubbish of various kinds have been brought by the currents and tides and built up around the edges of the Islet.

.51

San Servolo

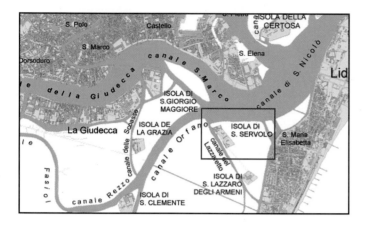

A community of Benedictine monks settled on the Island in 810 and built a church and monastery dedicated to St. Servolo. There was probably already a church dedicated to St. Christine before their arrival.

Forced to leave their convent in 1105, the Benedictine nuns of Sts. Leo and Basso were given permission to settle on the Island of St. Servolo. Their presence continued up to the early seventeenth century when owing to the state of bad repair of the buildings they were moved to the Convent of St. Mary the Humble in Venice (1615).

After having been used as a corn store and lazaretto, in 1647 the Senate granted permission to inhabit the Island to the nuns who had fled the Island of Candia . These nuns stayed on till 1715. Throughout their occupancy only minor maintenance works were carried out on the buildings.

With the nunnery practically vacant, in 1716 the Republic decided to use the buildings as a military hospital, assigning it to the care of the Hospitallers of St. John of God. Only essential alterations were made.

In 1733 the Island was turned over to the Fathers of St. John. The Church and Convent were fully renovated in line with the requirements of a hospital. Giovanni Scalfarotto was appointed building foreman (curator). The hospital was subsequently used for a growing number of mental patients, being wholly given over to this use in 1797.

In 1803 the buildings were extended to accommodate an increasing number of patients. The facility was converted into a mental asylum for inmates from the provinces of the Veneto.
Around the 1820s the Island itself was enlarged. The buildings underwent extensive renovation between 1846 and 1858.
Another bout of reclamation works prior to 1887 broadened the Island to its current size, as may be seen in a contemporary Military Engineer Corp survey map. Shortly after 1911 several cloister wings were torn down.

In 1932 the St. Servolo facility was taken over by the Provincial Government and the number of inmates started diminishing. Several new buildings were also erected.

The Province closed down the hospital in 1978. The facilities were in any case put to good use for a number of study and research activities as well as institutional activities.

In 1980 the Province undertook the restoration of historically noteworthy buildings on the Island.

Lido airport

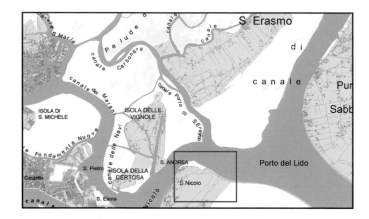

Nicelli airport in Lido

In the 1930s Nicelli was the second most important domestic airport and the first to have international cargo flights. By the end of World War II, though, it had ceased being a civil airport.

Nicelli's revival was not far off, however; its proximity to the city centre and the growing number of small tourist aircrafts made it once more attractive.

It is now open all year round for domestic flights and from April to October for international ones.

What's more, even before its come back the continued activity of the prestigious Aeroclub based at Nicelli has made its flying and parachuting school famous.

The Venetians and their boats

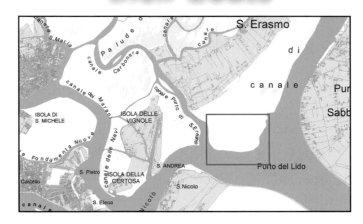

That doesn't mean though that the average inhabitant of the city owns a good-looking and well cared for boat. Indeed, not even that every Venetian owns a boat! As a matter of fact, only a few are lucky enough to have one at all. If nothing else because there wouldn't be enough room to fit them all in as the canals are too narrow and, not unlike for cars on the mainland, there's very little parking space, essentially only at the Giudecca.

Come Saturday evening, boat-equipped Venetians sail out to some restaurant-endowed Island to enjoy a good meal and some merrymaking in friendly company.

If Saturday night hasn't been spent stranded in the boat, come Sunday the Venetian may be seen sunbathing at the "bacan", a sort of beach between Venice and Point Sabbioni reachable only by boat.

il bacan

San Giorgio Maggiore

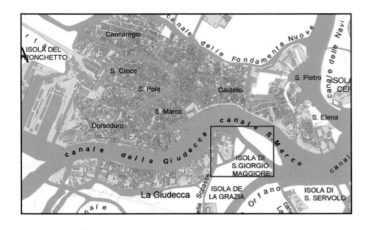

The Basilica of San Giorgio Maggiore on the Islet of the same name in Venice is the work of Andrea Palladio.

The façade has only one entrance flanked by four giant, plinth-supported columns topped by a classical tympanum-bearing beam, as in a temple with a four-pillared portico. The temple motif is picked up again at the rear where the pediment rests on an only slightly protruding lintel supported by pilaster strips.

Palladio outdid himself on this façade in terms of inventiveness and originality. Here was the solution to a problem Renaissance architects had long been struggling with, and namely how to bestow the appearance of a classical temple of antiquity on the façade of a building with a three-partitioned ground-plan, such as a triple-naved Christian church. Palladio effortlessly combined two temple-like front views, one for the centre nave and a smaller split one for the two side naves.

The building itself was completed in 1576, while the façade had to wait till 1610, that is thirty years after Palladio's demise, for completion by Vincenzo Scamozzi.

The advent of Napoleon and the fall of the Venetian Republic did not spare the Monastery, which lost all its privileges and ended up being used as a weapons store. Such defiling military applications continued for a century under French, Austrian, and even Italian dominion.

A contemporary monk has left us with a chronicle of the sad fate of the Island in which we appraise that "the Italian Government refuses to acknowledge the monks' hospice but has appointed a rector for the Temple's upkeep and for Holy Office.

The Island's fate has thus been sealed, as has that of the works of art and literature collected and cared for by the monks and held in safe keeping in its magnificent buildings. But of all this, modern-day progress leaves us nought save, out of its graciousness, the memory of having had these treasures in our midst."

After Second World War the Government granted St. George Major to the Cini Foundation which undertook works to restore to the Island part of its lost dignity. Thanks to the presence and commitment of this prominent institution the Island has become an important venue for renowned international cultural events.

Giudecca island

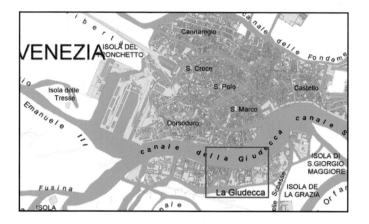

Giudecca is Venice's largest island.

Located south of the rest of the city, it hosts a peaceful residential neighbourhood. The long pier to the north towards the city affords an excellent promenade with wonderful views of the city amidst the lagoon.

The Island was once called "Spina Longa" (Long Fish Bone) for its elongated shape reminiscent of a fish bone. According to some, the presence on the Island of the first Jewish ghetto, which was subsequently moved to Cannareggio, accounts for its current name. Other sources maintain it derives from "Zudegà" (Judged), reference in this case being made to seditious aristocratic families banished here in the early ninth century.

In the days of the glorious Republic the Giudecca was a very pleasant, "far-from-the-maddening crowd" and extensively landscaped neighbourhood with fine, luxury dwellings.

The striking Church of the Redeemer still stands, witnessing to the magnificence of which those times were especially capable. The Church was in fact built between 1577 and 1592 in thanksgiving for the end of a plague that had struck the city in 1576 causing the death of a third of its population.

Each year the city's Chief Magistrate, the Doge, and his retinue would cross over to the Church from the so-called Zattere (Rafts) on wooden planks resting on a string of boats for the annual Feast Day of the Redeemer, which is still commemorated today on the third weekend of July.

Unlike the very rich and ornate interiors typical of many other Venetian churches, that of the Redeemer is sober in its neo-classical poise. The sacristy hosts several paintings by the great painter Paolo Veronese.

The best general view of this admirable late Renaissance Church may be had from the long pier south of the district (sestiere) of Dorsoduro in front of the Giudecca known as the Zattere (Rafts).

The Redeemer is not the only Palladian church on the Island. In fact, the Church of the Maidens (Zitelle) stands close by. It is open for morning Mass on Sundays and also hosts the most modern conference hall and facilities in Venice.

The adjacent building was once a convent for impoverished girls of rare beauty who could here learn traditional handicrafts, such as the famous Venetian lace.

The Gothic-revival ruins at the west end of the Island belong to the Stucky Flour Mill built in 1895 and discontinued in 1954. (See picture on the left)

One of the most luxurious Venetian mansions, Hotel Cipriani, is on the opposite side of the Island.

The Giudecca is currently been extensively renovated. Until recently it was pitifully decayed and even ill-reputed. Its narrow and dark alleyways, its dilapidated buildings, all contributed to making it a sort of Venetian "Bronx". Today, the Island is the scenario of many innovative residential complexes combining the latest novelties with the recovery of abandoned industrial establishments. Not surprisingly, the neighbourhood is much coveted by artists and intellectuals.

San Marco

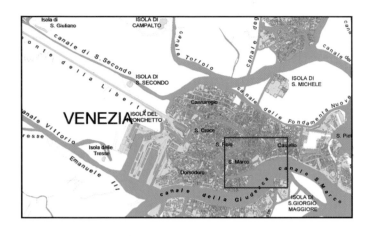

"*There, before him once more, lay the landing-place beyond description, the dazzling overall vision of fantastic buildings with which the Serenissima was wont to meet the incoming sailor's stunned gaze. The sparkling nimbleness of the Palace and of the Bridge of Sighs, the two columns on the embankment with the lion and saint, the glittering side of the fabulous temple, the view of the arch and clock of the Moors.*"

"*This was Venice, an alluring and allusive beauty, a fabled city and a snare for strangers...*"

Thomas Mann "Death in Venice" (editorial translation)

St. Mark's Basilica is a treasure-house of art and the scenario of many a history-making event. Its majestic façade and interior make up a unique showcase harbouring and exhibiting the masterpieces of great Italian and European artists who have worked here over the centuries.

Its extensive mosaics depicting the story of St. Mark and episodes of the First and Second Testament underscore the Basilica's Byzantine style.

The Basilica has always been a showcase of Venice's wealth, prosperity and magnificence. Over the centuries the Venetians have beautified and enriched the Basilica with precious artefacts and works of art from places far and wide, making for today's stunningly compact monument.

The soft, enveloping light greeting the visitor upon entry seems to separate the natural from the supernatural worlds, the latter glittering down from the gilded mosaics adorning the vaulted ceiling.
The Basilica overflows with art works, religious and iconographical motifs and symbols witnessing to the Basilica's role over the centuries. As abundant as they be, there's a thematic rationale running through them and they may be appreciated at different levels of comprehension.

Sadly, given the large crowds daily pouring into the Basilica, only a small portion of the art treasures of this universal gem are currently accessible to the visitor. The present site affords the opportunity of gaining a thorough knowledge of the Basilica's contents and of the deep religious meaning of its decorations and artefacts, all too easily overlooked in a cursory visit.

The first Church dedicated to St. Mark was a temporary building erected on the site of the present Ducal Palace. It was built in 828 when the Venetian merchants acquired the relics of St. Mark the Evangelist in Alexandria in Egypt.

Shortly after, in 832, a more permanent structure was erected on the site of the current Basilica. This building, though, was gutted by fire during a rebellion in 976 and was replaced in 978 by a new church.
The base of the current Basilica dates back to 1063. Rich spoils from the sack of Constantinople during the Fourth Crusade were brought back to augment the Basilica's treasure. The new adornments greatly enhanced its prestige. One of the most outstanding items was the famous bronze statues of the four horses, taken directly from the race-course of the Capital of the Eastern Roman Empire. The originals may now be admired in the Basilica's museum, the ones over the main doorway being replicas.

Two finely wrought columns salvaged from the Basilica of St. Polieuctus are incorporated in the right wall of St. Mark's Basilica

The Ducal Palace is one of Venice's unmistakable symbols.
It was presumably built between the tenth and eleventh centuries and erected over a pre-existing central, fortified rectangular structure with corner towers. One of Venice's Gothic-style masterpieces was to grow and develop out of this nucleus.

The first extensive renovation works were undertaken by the incumbent Chief Magistrate, Doge Sebastiano Ziani, in the twelfth century, thus turning the primitive fortress into a refined palace without any trace of its military past.
An extension was put in by the late thirteenth century.

The building as we see it today began to take shape under the government of Doge Bartolomeo Gradenigo (1339 – 1343).

Doge Francesco Foscari had the palace extended on the St. Mark's Basilica side in 1424. An important addition, the so-called Paper Doorway (Porta della Carta) designed by the architects Giovanni and Bartolomeo Bon (the same architects of Cà d'Oro), was completed in 1442.

The innermost part of the Palace, that is the "Rio di Palazzo" wing stretching back as far as the so-called Straw Bridge (Ponte della Paglia) where the Chief Magistrates apartments were located, was built after the great fire of 1483 to the design of the architect Antonio Rizzo. The sixteenth century was to witness an alternation of beautifying improvements, such as the Giant's Stairway and Alberghetti's Well, and devastating fires.

The so-called New Prisons building on the other side of the "rio" was designed by the architect Antonio Contin and erected in the early seventeenth century. This building was the headquarters of the so-called "Signori di notte al criminal", officials in charge of preventing and repressing criminal offences.

The New Prisons and the Ducal Palace were linked by the so-called Bridge of Sighs (Ponte dei Sospiri). After being condemned, prisoners were escorted from the Ducal Palace across the Bridge to the New Prisons.
After the fall of the Venetian Republic in 1797 the Palace ceased being used as the residence of the Chief Magistrate and of other government officials. The premises were put to use as public offices, but the so-called "Piombi" (Leads) Prisons continued as before. The Palace underwent considerable restoration after Venice's annexation to the Kingdom of Italy; in 1923 it was put to use as a museum and is still used as such today.

L'Arsenale

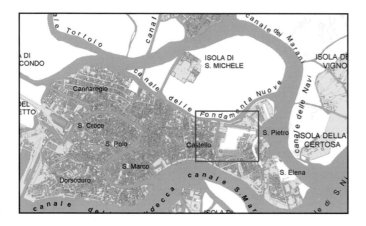

The Arsenal accounts for a good slice of the city. From the twelfth century onwards, the city's shipyards were chiefly based here. It's where the Serenissima drew its lifeblood; thanks to the daunting navy vessels built here, Venice was able to hold the Turks at bay in the Aegean Sea and gain control of the sea lanes of Northern Europe.

As the largest centrally controlled production plant of the pre-industrial age, the Arsenal may justly be considered the first factory in the world. Only a small part is currently being used as one of the Biennial's exhibition venue and as a light-duty shipyard.

The Arsenal stretched over an area of forty-six hectares. At the peak of production it employed from between 1,500 to 2,000 journeymen (Arsenalotti). Indeed, at one stage the payroll records up to 4,500 to 5,000, corresponding to between two and five percent of the overall urban population, which at the time (XII century) was around 100,000 inhabitants.

The first systematic shipyards were established by order of the Chief Magistrate, Doge Ordelafo Faliero, to meet the strategic naval requirements of the ever more prosperous expanding Republic in 1104.

Siting of the Arsenal between the Convents of St. Peter of the Castle and the Parish Church of St. John in Bragora (Old Dock) was due to both strategic and logistic reasons (easier defence against any enemy attack in the former case and easier unloading of incoming timber from the mainland forests in Cadore in the latter). Records dating to the early thirteenth century mention two rows of boat-sheds on either embankment of the Old Dock. These may be considered as the core of the Arsenal. Access to this area from St. Mark's Dock could only be had across a narrow canal.

By the early twelfth century the city's naval demands had increased considerably. "St. Daniel's Lake" by the Monastery of the same name was added and the New Arsenal constructed in the New Dock. After these extensions, Venice's shipyard facilities covered a surface area of 138,000 square metres. Another later addition was the "Stradal Campagna", where the current casting houses, oar workshops, Tana rope factory, and the artillery works were sited.

The earthen portal of monumental proportions was erected in 1453 after the fall of Constantinople and the increasing threat of Turkish dominion in the Mediterranean. The structure was meant to allude to Venice's role as a bulwark of Christianity. The portal is flanked by two towers, later rebuilt in the fifteenth century. Classical Roman triumphal arches served as a model for the portal, which may be considered the first Renaissance-style construction in the city.

The Arsenal continued growing for almost a century between 1473 and 1570. This third stage of the Arsenal's expansion saw the addition of dwellings for the workers outside the yards along with public bread-ovens, corn stores (the Newest Dock), and moorings for the galleasses, bringing the surface area covered by the Arsenal to almost twenty-four hectares. Architecturally noteworthy is the Gagiandre boat-house erected in 1570, possibly to a design by Jacopo Sansovino.

The rope factories were sited in a new area called Tana. It was here that this vitally important commodity for shipping was produced on an industrial scale at the lowest possible costs. The self-sufficiency achieved by the Republic in this type of production was an advantage all the more appreciated in case of war. The raw material (hemp, which was also used for caulking the hulls of the vessels) was chiefly imported from the estuary of the Don River on the Azov Sea. The Venetians had established excellent business relationships with suppliers in the area, thus guaranteeing the flawless quality of the supplies. Instead of processing to standard lengths, the finished ropes were made to come out of holes, where they were then cut to the desired length.

Such a system proved to be especially cost-saving and the ropes were even sold to ships in transit at prices well below those of the competition. The production of galleys and large barges at the Arsenal went on for three centuries surrounded by secrecy. The Battle of Levanto in 1571 was largely won thanks to the war-galleys built here. Without a doubt the Arsenal was the hub and heart of Venice's growth and success.

During the first period of French occupation (1797-1798) Napoleon scuttled all the vessels in the Arsenal except those that could be integrated in the French fleet for future battles. All the 2,000 journeymen were dismissed and the distinction between the merchant and war navy was abolished. The French also carried out works at the Arsenal to improve its accessibility by opening the Porta Nuova (New Gate) canal and erecting the tower of the same name.

The layout of the Arsenal was also partially rearranged by the Austrians during their first Government between 1798 and 1806. The second French Government carried out structural alterations to permit resumption of work at the yards and upgrade productivity.

In the fourth and last stage of the shipyard's major development between 1876 and 1909 the Italian Government planned to use the Arsenal as an important naval base in the Upper Adriatic. The Arsenal was hence further extended to incorporate new areas including the large open space in front of the docks known as "Piazzale dei Bacini" and those of the three suppressed convents of St. Daniel, the Virgins, and Celestia. Following on several projects aimed at increasing ship manoeuvrability space the existing infrastructures between the new and newest dockyards were demolished and the current large dock excavated. Ground level was slightly raised by about 70 cm to avoid submersion.

No longer capable of meeting the ever increasing requirements of a modern navy, over the following years the Arsenal slowly declined to the point of being almost completely abandoned. In recent years attempts have been made to recover the Arsenal by using it as a venue for cultural events. The debate as to its possible utilization is still open but given the extent of the area concerned no easy solution seems to be forthcoming.

Passenger Terminal

VENEZIA

Venice's passenger terminal is the leading home port in the Mediterranean.

Mediterranean cruises departing from and returning to Venice are a consolidated reality. Cruise statistics show Venice to have been a leading cultural and tourist destination of great appeal in recent years.

Since 1997 passenger traffic at the Port of Venice has been handled by the Venezia Terminal Passeggeri S.p.A. on behalf of the local port authority.
The nautical and technical facilities and services offered by this company are among the best anywhere in the Mediterranean.
In 2005 passenger traffic peaked at a record figure of 1,365,375 (+31.6% over 2004)

corresponding to a total of 1,414 landings.

The cruise season has been brought forward to January and the success of these winter cruises has resulted in an increase in tourist traffic and in the number of shipping companies operating out of Venice in a traditionally off-season period.
In 2005 this increase amounted to 447 more landings and 815,153 more passengers.

2005 was also the record year for ferries with 446,376 passengers corresponding to an increase of 77.5% compared to 2004.

The Port of Venice hence confirms itself as first choice for passengers travelling to Greece and East Mediterranean countries.

Fort Sant'Andrea

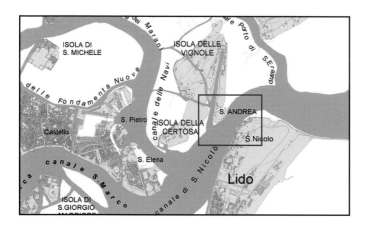

Fort St. Andrew was built in the mid sixteen century on the ruins of pre-existing defence works. The Fort was designed by the Verona-born architect Michele Sanmicheli (1484-1559) who was assigned by the Venetian Government the task of building artillery emplacements to prevent access from the sea of any enemy fleet in what was considered an especially weak point.

The Fort is sited at the tip of Vignole Island. It features a central body built on the remains of a pre-existing fifteen century keep and an outer bastion at the base of which the guns were located.

The rectangular embrasures in the bastion were almost level with the water surface so as to direct gunfire horizontally as close as possible to enemy ship waterline.
A long casemate with vaulted ceiling surmounted by a rampart used as ammunition store is still to be found inside the bastion.

When the Fort was built artillery had already evolved considerably. Contemporary guns had in fact a smaller calibre and were capable of longer shots at reduced angles, that is shots far straighter than those of the bombards used in the previous century.

A corridor runs through the middle of the casemate connecting the bastion with the inner courtyard at the end of which, on the courtyard side, there are two seats for the pins of a hoist used for delivering the ammunition. It appears that the bastion and the casemate were once connected by a vault subsequently demolished.

Access to the Fort is on the opposite side of the bastion. Rear access to the Fort was protected by a ditch separating the landing from the courtyard. While heavily armed in front, the Fort was completely unarmed at the rear.

This denotes great confidence in the Fort's fire power. In fact, with its forty guns with various firing angles it must have been deemed very difficult for any vessel to get behind the Fort. The Fort was not conceived of for short-distance defence but was meant to keep any enemy well at bay.

Formally speaking the structure is extremely interesting as a whole. The most pleasant architectural feature, though, is the front with the large door at the centre and two side arches of equal size.

A commemorative inscription on the front of the keep topped by the lion of St. Mark is dedicated to the Battle of Lepanto. The keep itself is topped by a terrace which, given the nature of its pavement, would appear to have been designed to collect water, funnelling it off through a hole at the centre.

An interesting flag- or standard- pole holder in Istria stone is set in the wall on the windward side.

Until recently the Fort was still being used as a barracks.
A lot of work was subsequently put in to off-set its continual subsistence. A sub-foundation was laid the external border of which may be seen just below water mark at a few metres from the boundary of the Fort. This remedial action has indeed prevented the Fort from falling down.

Despite the resources expended for its consolidation, no decision has unfortunately yet been made as to possible utilisation.

For the moment it may only be reached by privately operated boats. The Island is in any case overgrown and in a sorry state of utter neglect.

Rather than being concerned that the Fort see action, its builders meant its conspicuous power to impress visitors and ambassadors, especially from the Ottoman Empire, confident that the sight of its might alone would be dissuasive. In fact, after the worst had passed and the fear of an attack had been allayed, the Fort was manned by merely representative garrisons.

We've been left an interesting description of the complex and of the life that went on in the Fort in the memoirs of the Venetian adventurer and writer, Giacomo Casanova, who was detained here between March and July 1743. Strictly speaking the Fort was not a gaol but an ideal place for keeping troublesome individuals out of harms way instead of imprisoning them.

Maximiliam Tower in Sant'Erasmo

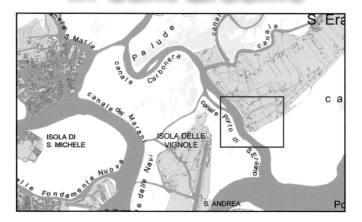

The ancient and powerful Maximilian Tower broods over the small beach of 'bacan', where the Venetians traditionally go to bathe or for a picnic. No longer an eminent ruin of Austrian military architecture dating to 1800, it is now a very real physical presence, a prominent feature with a life of its own and capable of livening up its surroundings on the once frontline of fire that defended the Lagoon.

It derives its name from Archduke Maximilian of Austria who took refuge here during the fierce uprisings of 1848. It has been completely restored by the Venice Magistrato alle Acque according to a project drawn up by the architects Carlo Cappai and Maria Alessandra Segantini.

The works were carried out as part of a more general urban upgrading and high-waters protection plan. After many years of neglect and decay, the green Island renowned for its vegetable gardens and vineyards has finally recovered its most notable monument.

Indeed, Fort Erasmus or Fort Maximilian, also referred to in the more place-name documents as "Maximilian Tower", on the south-west tip of the Island of St. Erasmus before Port Lido, is a nineteenth century stronghold quite unlike any other military fortification of the detached maritime stronghold fortresses of the Venetian Lagoon.

It is worth noting that till the fall of the Venetian Republic in 1797 there were only a few forts defending the Lagoon. These were essentially sited before the port mouths and included Forte San Nicolò and Sant'Andrea at the mouth of the St. Mark Basin and, along the southern reaches of the Lagoon, in addition to the Octagons, Forts Alberoni, San Pietro, San Felice. , Brondolo and San Michele. Practically no defence was envisaged on the leeward side of the Lagoon except for the Castle of Mestre. This was because the mainland cities had sworn their allegiance to Venice since the fourteenth century so that the city on the Lagoon felt safe on this side.

The full-scale militarisation of the Lagoon began in 1797, initially under the French, followed by the Austrian till 1866, and then by the Italian army up to 1945. Over this period the Lagoon was turned into a maritime stronghold made up of a string of detached fortresses. Indeed, it was among the most extensive military strongholds of Italy, together with the Verona-Peschiera Quadrilateral and that of Rome, with military commands and barracks occupying every suppressed convent of the city and almost all the islands. By 1945 there were little below a hundred fortified and garrisoned detachments in the Lagoon.

It was during this "modern" stage after 1797 that the Fort on the shore of St. Erasmus Island was erected as part of the more general progressive upgrading of the defence system as a whole and in particular of the reinforcement of the military facilities protecting Port Lido.

.83

San Secondo

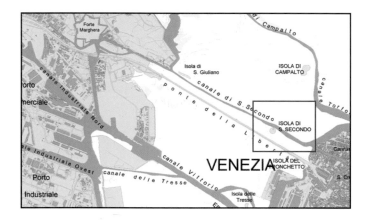

A church to host the holy image of St. Erasmus was built under the patronage of the Baffo family in 1034. A community of Benedictine nuns established itself in the adjacent convent.

In 1237 the relics of St. Secundus were brought to the Island from Asti, thus giving it the name by which it is still known today.
The Benedictine nuns were replaced by the Dominican Fathers in 1533.

During a plague epidemic in 1566 the Island was put to use as a lazaretto.

Following on a fire at the Arsenal in 1569, the Senate ordered that keeps be erected on a number of islands in the Lagoon for use as powder-stores. The one on St. Secundus was the first to be built.
Following on the Napoleonic decree of 1806 in which several ecclesiastical orders and institutions were abolished, the Dominicans withdrew to the Jesuits' Convent.

In 1824 the buildings were demolished and the Island was occupied by a military garrison. Sometime in the twentieth century the Island was turned over to the State and placed in the care of a private family.

Today, the Island is completely deserted; the ruins of a redoubt probably dating to the second half of the nineteenth century may still be seen.

The Liberty Bridge

Venice was built up on islands and sandbars in the middle of the Venetian Lagoon, halfway between the mainland and the open sea.
Till 1846 the only access was by boat. Then, an almost four kilometre-long railway bridge was opened that year.

Plans were soon afoot to build a road bridge, but its realization had to wait until 1933 when the bridge now called "Liberty Bridge" was finally opened.
This perfectly straight and flat (except the last kilometre on the Venice side) bridge is 3,580 metres long. It is essentially the last stretch of National Highway 11, the so-called Upper Po Valley Highway.

Liberty bridge is the only automobile access route to the city. About 70,000 people come in this way each day. On a heavy traffic day, the Bridge may be crossed by up to as many as 30,000 vehicles.

.85

San Michele

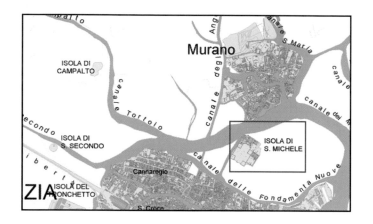

A church dedicated to San Michele Arcangelo was built on the Island under the patronage of the Briosa and Brustolana families sometime in the tenth century. Tradition has it that St. Romuald, founder of the Order of Camaldoli, spent several years here as a hermit.

In 1424 the hallowed place was assigned to Giovanni Brunaccci of the Order of St. Brigid by the city's Chief Magistrate, Doge Foscari.
In 1435 the Island was turned over to the Augustine Order of Mount Ortone and the Church was rebuilt.

Building of the so-called "small" cloister, which is still extant, was begun in 1436. The bell-tower was erected between 1456 and 1460. Several years after Abbot Pietro Donà commissioned the rebuilding of the Church to Mauro Codussi. Work went on from 1468 to 1480, with the two chapels adjacent the presbytery being built between 1475 and 1480. Part of the monastic buildings were also restructured in the course of these works.

Building of the polygon-shaped Emiliana Chapel designed by Guglielmo Bergamasco gets under way in 1528 to the wishes of the widow of the patrician Giovanni Emiliani. In 1575 an outbuilding on the west side of the square in front of the Church for use as a boat-house (cavana) was added to the convent complex. No further alterations are recorded in the seventeenth and eighteenth century prints still extant.

Following on Napoleonic decrees suppressing ecclesiastical institutions and orders, in 1807 the friars moved to St. Stephen's Convent in Venice. Three years later all buildings on the Island were demolished and the Island was set to use as a cemetery by order of Napoleon. A fully enclosing wall with the insertion of an octagon-shaped chapel was built around the cemetery.

In 1818 negotiations to purchase the Islands of St. Michael and St. Christopher were undertaken with the Government by the Venice City Council with a view to using them as municipal burial grounds. A Military Engineer Corps survey map dated 1887 shows the set up to be not unlike the one prevailing today, which is the outcome of extensive reclamation works and an overall redesign. The extensive reclamation works on the Eastern side of the two Islands are recorded for the first time in a document dated 1908.

The Island as it now stands is the result of further works throughout the twentieth century.

Lazzaretto Nuovo

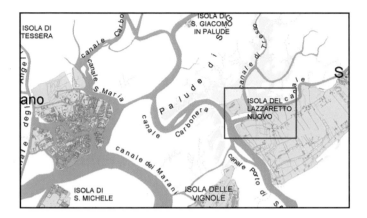

The Island is first mentioned in a donation deed dated 1015. The deed also specifies the presence of a large vineyard. In 1107 the Island became the property of the monks of the Monastery of St. George Major, who held on to it up to the Napoleonic suppressions. Throughout their tenure, the Island was rented out to various private parties.

A small hospice and church dedicated to St. Bartholomew were built sometime between 1300 and 1400.

In 1468 the Senate ordered the construction of a Lazaretto for the quarantine of goods and preventive custody as a precautionary measure against the risk of spreading infectious diseases. It was qualified as "Novo" (New) to distinguish it from the other Lazaretto then extant at the Lido where overtly diseased patients were interned. There were small detached dwellings inside the four-sided compound with the vineyard still in the middle.

Between the mid sixteenth and early seventeenth centuries the buildings were extended or rebuilt and the vineyard taken out to make room for the large goods shelters (tesoni). The perimeter of the complex was also extended. The Island as it now stands appears in a drawing by G.A. Cornello dated 1687.

In 1562 the Big Teson (shelter) was built to lay out textiles for cleansing. Over the eighteenth century the condition of the Island progressively deteriorated; the canals filled in and the buildings grew derelict.

By order of the Republic the Newest Lazaretto was opened on Poveglia in 1793. Over the centuries the buildings of this Lazaretto were used sporadically and are currently dilapidated.

After the Napoleonic suppressions in the early nineteenth century the Island was turned over to military applications. It was first used as a powder depot and then fortified with earthworks and bastions beyond the original enclosure.

In 1975 the Lazaretto was evacuated by the army and turned over to a volunteer association (Ekos Club). The two sixteenth century powder-stores of the New Lazaretto were restored some ten years ago under the supervision of the Architectural Heritage and Environmental Protection Agency of Venice.

The stores have recently been re-appointed. Display cases and exhibition facilities have been set up in the eastside store and a library-cum-records collection in the smaller westside store.

.89

Trezze island

Trezze Island is a former artillery emplacement in a defence line of seven (later eight), polygon-shaped batteries strung out across the Lagoon between Venice and mainland Mestre.

The emplacements were originally built on pile-work platforms driven into shallow water beds or sandbars, often in proximity to canal intersections.

In a letter dated 1797 signed by Zuanne Zusto, a nobleman and official in charge of the surveillance and upkeep of the Lagoon and beaches ("Provveditore"), reference is made to works of the previous year, from which it appears that seven wooden forts for the defence of Venice had already been built.

By 1883 all artillery emplacements in the Lagoon have been converted to earthwork structures with ramparts, magazines and small barracks.

Two types of earthwork batteries, one larger and the other smaller, both, though, of the same shape (seven short sides forming a semi-circle and a long side) are recorded in Austrian High Command reports in Vienna dated 1900. All batteries are recorded as having battlements, small barracks and gun-powder stores. The documents also mention the presence of artificial reefs protecting stockade embankments.

In 1975 Trezze Island was licensed out to VeneziaGas (currently ITALGAS S.p.A.). Fully automated natural gas distribution facilities were

Murano

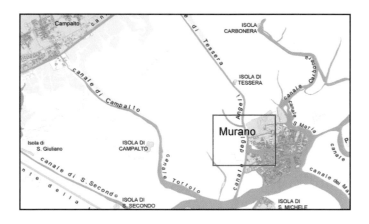

Murano Island lies north-east of Venice along the Marani Canal. Its population runs to about six thousand inhabitants. It is in actual fact made up of seven islets separated by channels and canals crossed by bridges.

Its most notable monuments include the Venetian-Byzantine-style Church of Sts. Mary and Donatus originally built in the seventh century and renovated in the twelfth and St. Peter Martyr built between the fifteenth and sixteenth centuries. The latter hosts paintings by Paolo Veronese and Giovanni Bellini as well as the magnificent Chapel of the Ballarin family of Murano, which may be admired in the right wing of the Church.

The Island is synonymous with fine glassware the world over, be it blown, cut, or lamp-blown.

Thanks to this craft and its vicinity to Venice, Murano is a favourite destination for scores of tourists.

San Giacomo in Paludo

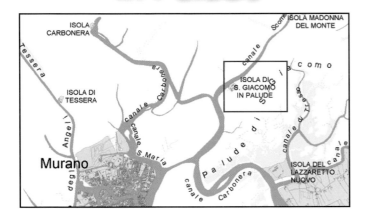

In 1046 some marshland was granted to Giovanni Trono of Mazzorbo by the Chief Magistrate, Doge Orso Badoer, for the erection of a convent to host pilgrims and travellers, dedicated to St. James Major.

Following on the arrival of Cistercian nuns in 1238 alterations were made to the Convent and the rim of the Island extended thanks to further grants by the Church of Murano.
After a period of decline, in 1440 the nuns moved to the Convent of St. Margaret of Torcello leaving the Island deserted.

During a plague epidemic in 1456 lepers from St. Lazarus were put up on the Island for a time.

After being deserted for spell the Island was settled by a religious community of the Franciscan Order of the Convent Minors. The friars undertook the construction of a new small church and convent, a guesthouse, and other minor outbuildings, renting out the vegetable garden and vineyard to private parties.

The once extensive Convent was reported in 1696 as having only five rooms, a sizeable guesthouse, and a capacious covered boathouse and porch for mariners in distress.

By the eighteenth century the boathouse was slowly falling to pieces, clearly calling for urgent measures to reclaim it and the surrounding area to public use.

In 1778 the Island was considered as a viable depot for stockpiling all of the Republic's gunpowder, all the more so as the monastery was no longer in use. The plan was scrapped, though, given the high costs and long lead times entailed.

Following on the Napoleonic decree suppressing religious orders in 1810, the monastery and church were demolished.

Between the second half of the nineteenth and early twentieth centuries a redoubt and garrison were based on the Island.
Three powder-magazines duly detached and shielded by an equal number of embankments and other buildings to service the garrison were built and may still be seen today.
The Island was evacuated by the army in 1961.

After being neglected for some time, one of the large military sheds, suitably refitted for the occasion, was used by the Venice Biennale in the summer of 1975 for fringe performances.

In 1993 the boathouse, boundary wall and two buildings overlooking the canal linking Murano and Burano were restored by the Inland Waterways Authority (Magistrato alle Acque).

The Island is currently deserted and except for the buildings and works restored in 1993, all other constructions are derelict.

San Francesco nel Deserto

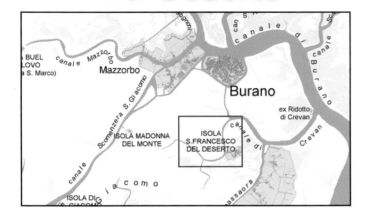

The Island's owner, Giacomo Michieli, had a church erected here dedicated to St. Francis of Assisi in 1228, shortly after the Saint's canonisation. Tradition has it that the Saint briefly sojourned on the Island on his return from the Holy Land in 1220, erecting a shelter next to an already existing oratory.

In 1233 Michieli donated the Island to the Franciscan friars Minor who proceeded to build a convent. The friars had to vacate the Island, though, owing to deteriorating climatic conditions in the Lagoon.
The Island was to remain uninhabited between 1420 and 1453, a circumstance that, it is believed, deserved it its designation "in the Desert".

In 1453 the Island was donated by Pope Pius II to the Observant Friars Minor who set about restoring the Church and Convent and adding on a Renaissance-style cloister.

A community of Reformed Friars Minor dispatched to the Island by Pope Clement VIII in 1594 upgraded its guest facilities, planted a great number of cypress trees, extended the choir, and restored the refectory. In 1683 the Senate granted the friars permission to build a wooden bridge to join the Island to St. Erasmus.

The fresco wall paintings were despoiled by French troops during the sack of Venice in 1799. The Convent was suppressed in 1806 and the complex was put to use as a powder-magazine. Guns were also installed on the Island at this time.

In 1856 the Island was donated by the Austrian Emperor, Francis Joseph, to the Patriarch of Venice, who placed it in the permanent care of the Franciscan Friars Minor. The friars restored the two cloisters and rebuilt the Church; important reclamation and hydraulic engineering works were also carried out at this time.

The original Church facade and the inside of the nave were revived by the Monuments Preservation Authority (Sovrintendenza ai Monumenti) of Venice in 1943.

The Island was enlarged in 1950 by reclaiming part of the sandbar to the west. The canal that currently makes its way into the Island, once continued on cutting the Island off from the surrounding sandbars.

Further restorations were carried out between 1961 and '63 along with an intensive archaeological campaign that led to the reconstruction of the presbytery apse and dome.

Carbonera and Tessera

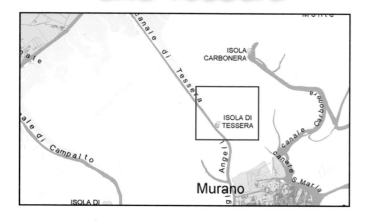

The Islands of Tessera and Carbonera were former artillery emplacements in a defence line of seven (later eight), polygon-shaped batteries strung out across the Lagoon between Venice and mainland Mestre.

The eight batteries included: Fisolo, Campana, Ex Poveglia and lastly Trezze barring the Lagoon's southern approaches; Campalto, Tessera, Carbonera, Buel del Lovo or Battery San Marco in the centre of the Lagoon and along its northern reaches.

The emplacements were originally built on wooden pile-work platforms driven into shallow water beds or sandbars, often in proximity to canal intersection.

The Campalto, Tessera and Carbonera are chronicled as being in earthwork already in 1848. The latter appears to have been repositioned during this alteration so as to align it with the batteries at Tessera and St. Mark (Buel del Lovo).

By 1883 all artillery emplacements in the Lagoon had been converted to earthwork structures with ramparts, magazines and small barracks.

In the early twentieth century a wireless telegraph station of the Italian Navy was installed on Carbonera Island. Not far from the shack, reinforced concrete pedestals upon which the aerials once rested may still be seen edging up out of the water. The still extant buildings date back to this period.

In the second half of the twentieth century Tessera Island was taken over by a private concern. Since then new residential complexes were progressively built and existing buildings restored.

Carbonera Island is instead totally deserted and its buildings are dilapidated.

Carbonera

Tessera

Mazzorbo

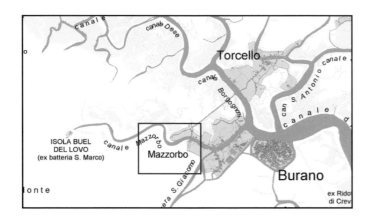

As a matter of fact, though, its Latin name, "Maiurbium", means "major city". It's a name that points to the Island's onetime importance as an emporium.

Despite being at the time narrower than what it is now, the Island hosted five parishes and five monasteries. Five monasteries, it should be noted, that like others in the Lagoon were not merely small backwater affairs but sizeable facilities intended to provide education for the offspring of the Venetian nobility and patrician families. As such, not surprisingly, they were also often the custodians of artistic masterpieces, such as those of Paolo Veronese.

Many monasteries and mansions have not fared too well at the hands of time and man (especially Napoleon's troops). Nevertheless, something has survived - for instance, the fourteenth century Church in a Romanesque-Gothic style of St. Catherine and several houses in the Gothic style strung out along the main canal.

A small curiosity: the bell in the Church's bell-tower is the oldest anywhere in the Lagoon and dates to 1318.

What's left of the redoubt may be seen in the top of the picture on the left. The redoubt stands on the site of the ancient monastery of St. Euphemia founded by a noblewoman of Padova in the year 900.

After the Monastery's suppression in 1786 the buildings were initially turned over to military use and then demolished in 1838 to make room for the redoubt, which was initially intended as a munitions store.

In 1909 the Italian Military High Command decided to demolish the redoubt and a reinforced concrete rampart with six gun pits was erected in its place.

The site was subsequently abandoned and was recently assigned to the Italian Catholic Guides' and Scouts' Association, in whose care it is still today.

Burano

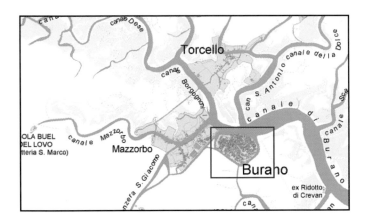

The Island lies south-east of Mazzorbo and with its 5,000 inhabitants is the most important settlement in the northern reaches of the Lagoon.

Heavily urbanised, the Island preserves little of its natural appearance.
Burano or Boreana takes its name from the gate of the city of Altino, of which it was once a colony. When Torcello was already ranked a city, Burano was its "vicus", that is to say a dependent hamlet.

Legend has it that after departing from his beloved at Murano a mariner reached an isle inhabited by sirens. While the rest of the crew jumped overboard to arrive at them, the mariner withstood their alluring chant. Amazed at such fidelity, the queen of the sirens struck the waters with her tail and up rose a crown of foam that then solidified turning into a bridal veil for the mariner's distant sweetheart. Since then the girls of the Island have striven to reproduce it with needle and thread.

The Island, at a distance of about nine kilometres from Venice, is unmistakable in its uniqueness. No imposing building meets the eye of the incoming visitor, who is nevertheless pleasantly greeted by an attractive skyline of uniform, equally high houses of different colours.

The at most two storey-high buildings with their look-alike facades and simple square windows are indeed of rustic mien. If it weren't for their different colours it would be hard to distinguish them. Yellow, green, red, sky blue…. these are the colours the women of the Island used to paint their houses in when their men-folk were out to sea so that when they returned they could already make it out from afar as they came in.

Notwithstanding what was said above regarding the unassuming architecture of the town, noteworthy buildings did once exist, only a part of which has survived to this day. Until Napoleon's famous decree, there were four religious buildings on the Island dependant on the diocese of Torcello.
These included the still extant but no longer consecrated St. Mary of the Graces, also referred to as the Capuchins; St. Mauro; St. Vito; and the still extant parish Church of St. Martin Bishop. Their antiquity is witnessed to by records dating to the twelfth century in which they are already mentioned.

A monastery with seven inside oratories representing the seven major basilicas of Rome was annexed to St. Mary of the Graces, then known as St. Hadrianus.

St. Mauro, also referred to as St. Moro, was founded in 899. Seventh century manuscripts describe the Church as having three naves, the nuns' choir, and an ornate organ with paintings. The Church was reconstructed and newly consecrated for Holy Service in 1533.

The monastic establishment annexed to St. Vito must have been rather underprivileged. The Church had only one nave, three chapels, the nuns' choir, and was all very plain.

St. Mauro and St. Vito were suppressed in 1806. St. Martin Bishop was built in 1500 and afterwards variously restored. It still hosts seventeenth and eighteenth century paintings, among which the notable "Crucifixion", an early work by the young Tiepolo.

The most prominent native of Burano ("buranello") is Baldassarre Galuppi, a Baroque musician. The Island's main square has been named after him.

Not to be missed in the square is the School of Lacework.
Needlepoint lacework without any underlying supporting fabric is a speciality of the Island tracing its origins to the early sixteenth century.
Typical stitches are "punto in aria", "punto a rosette" and "punto controtagliato". The latter is chunkier and solemn in its ample bas-relief motifs.

The trade war sparked by France brought the craft to the verge of extinction. It was largely thanks to the unremitting efforts of an enterprising commoner, Cencia Scarpariola, that in the late nineteenth century the secrets of the fine craft were passed on to future generations and given a new lease of life.

Crevan

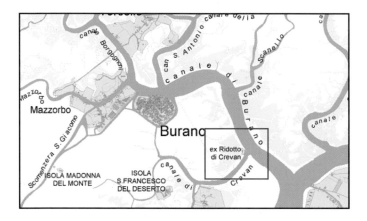

Of the nine island batteries defending the Lagoon, Crevan was the last to be built.

After handing over of Venetian territory to the French under the Treaty of Presburg in 1806, the new masters deemed the northern shores of the Lagoon to be under-defended and hence set about remedying the deficiency by building the artillery emplacement at Crevan.

The master plan drawn up by Label, an engineer and at the time Fortifications' Supervisor, envisaged the replacement of all wooden pile-work batteries with ones resting on solid ground duly protected by embankments, as well as the construction of a new emplacement, the Crevan redoubt, to defend the port of Treporti and the northern coastline of Cavallino in general.

In 1814 the Austrians were once more back in Venice and in control. It was only in response to the European-wide troubles of 1831 that upgrading of the city's defences was seriously tackled, though.

A high-ranking military committee of the city was assigned the task of overhauling the defences of the maritime stronghold. In addition to upgrading existing defences, the committee recommended new permanent works to be put up capable of holding off any future enemy attack.

The redoubt at Crevan also came up for refitting and between 1832 and 1842 a fortified barracks was built that may still be seen today.
When the Austrians once again occupied this part of Italy in 1849, the Venetian stronghold was the base for the Imperial Army's southern and eastern campaigns.

By 1865 the Lagoon stronghold had lost its strategic importance for the defence of the Veneto region and a special committee was appointed to decide on possible decommissioning and the Crevan emplacement was among those deemed obsolete.

The Austrians unsuccessfully attempted to quickly revive the maritime stronghold but too late, and in 1866 it, inclusive of the Crevan redoubt, was surrendered together with other occupied territory and incorporated in the Kingdom of Italy.

Under the new masters the fortifications in the Lagoon were strengthened.
The Island's recent history is not unlike many others in the Lagoon. As with these, after decommissioning it was granted for use to private concerns.

Over the years the new occupants have restored the buildings and generally ensured the upkeep of the Island.

Torcello

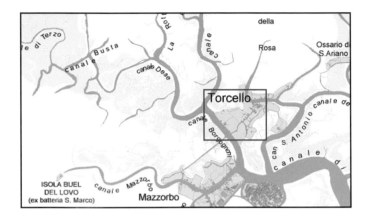

At the peak of its affluence the population of ancient Dorceum or Turricellum was close to 50,000 inhabitants.

Between 638 and 1689 it was the seat of a bishopric. Its period of greatest growth and wealth was during the High Middle Ages, when its was a leading port, also thanks to its three canals directly connected to the sea, and an extremely busy centre for the working of metal, glass and wool.

In 1272 it and its environs were indeed granted a monopoly for the milling of wool. In a tenth century chronicle, the Byzantine Emperor Costantino Porfirgenito remarks that Torcello is a great emporium.

By the fifteenth century, though, the Island had already begun its steady decline. Sixteen monasteries and many churches for a total of twelve parishes were reported as still steadfastly holding on despite the unfavourable circumstances. The initially partial and then total filling in of the port mouths, the sediments brought down by the Sile and Dese Rivers, the encroaching marshes, the prevalence of fresh over salt water, the curse of malaria, all joined forces to decree the Islands downfall.

The monumental complex is still extant, and namely the Cathedral, the Baptistery, and Ste. Fosca's Martyrium.

As already said, the Cathedral of Ste. Mary Assumption originated in the seventh century. By the High Middle Ages it had already undergone considerable alterations, the first in 864 and the second in 1008 when Orso Orseolo, the son of Pietro the Orseolo, was ordained bishop and appointed to Torcello.

The porch in front of the Cathedral, whose façade was raised around 1000, was extended in the fourteenth century. The shutters on the windows are quite unusual as they are made out of heavy marble slabs.

The three-nave interior hosts no mean number of artistic masterpieces, starting from the precious marble mosaic flooring, followed by the mosaic embellishing the semicircular wall of the apse and the Triumphal Arch, depicting the twelve Apostles, the Annunciation, and the so-called Teotoga Virgin. Other Ravenna- and Venetian-Byzantine-style mosaics may be admired adorning the apse on the right-hand side and above the main doorway. The latter, dating to the twelfth century, depict the Apotheosis of Christ and the Last Judgement.

After coming out from the Cathedral and visiting the Baptistery and the cross-shaped Church of Ste. Fosca with its surrounding octagon-shaped porch, the renowned and so-called "Attila's Throne" deserves a brief stop. The stone chair was in fact never used by the King of the Huns but by the Island officials called "tribunes" to met out justice.

Worth calling in is also the Estuary Museum, which houses an interesting collection of Medieval and modern archaeology artefacts.
One of the most notable exhibits is a gilded silver altar-piece dating to around the twelfth century. There are also many interesting inscriptions, statues, documents, earthenware, and weapons.

Ossario di S.Ariano

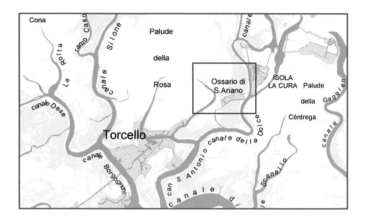

A cluster of islets separated by canals crossed by bridges was once scattered between Ammiana and Torcello. The larger was called Costanziaca and was first settled by citizens of Altino fleeing from the barbarian invasions of the fifth century. Its population grew to considerable proportions as did the number of its ecclesiastical buildings. The settlement was a dependency of Ammiana.

The leading church on the Island was that of St. Aryan. Founded in 1160, it quickly became the final resting place of many a member of the Venetian nobility and was considerably wealthy thanks to its many benefices.
Like for Ammiana, erosion set in and over the centuries Costanziaca gradually declined. By the mid 1400s it was evacuated by its last inhabitants.
What's left today is but a mere scrap of the former Island of Costanziaca.
Recent excavations have uncovered the remains of an extensive settlement on the right-hand side of "La Dolce" canal south of St. Aryan dating to the seventh century. Several foundations west of the charnel-house have been identified as the remains of the monastery.

Adverse environmental conditions induced the nuns of St. Aryan to abandon the Island and move to St. Angel of Zampenigo on Torcello in 1439.

Records witness to the Church of St. Aryan still being extant in 1510. With the buildings next to derelict, massive emission of fresh water into the Lagoon by the Sile River through its nearby estuary in the mid 1500s caused further damage to the environment, hence jeopardising the site's viability. It is in this period, in fact, that massive works were got underway to channel the estuaries of the main rivers discharging into the Lagoon directly out to sea.

The proposal put forward by the Sanitary Authorities to build a wall around the Island and use it as an ossuary for the human remains dug up out of the graveyards of Venice was approved by the Senate in 1556.

The cemetery and a small church next to the boundary wall probably built at the time the ossuary was established but currently no longer extant appear in a drawing by Tommaso Scalfurotto dated 1779.
This arrangement is borne out by other records, including historical land office maps.
The Island and ossuary are currently somewhat neglected. Not even the foundations of the old buildings are any longer visible.

La Cura

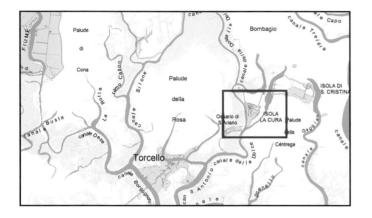

The history of La Cura Island is associated with that of an important group of islets once located between Ammiana and Torcello and collectively known as Costanziaca, which were settled in the fifth century by some of the inhabitants of Altino fleeing before the barbarian invasions.

Except for several recent archaeological finds, records, whether material or documentary, of La Cura are scanty. Five ecclesiastical establishments once stood east of Torcello, where only sandbars and mounds are now to be found. Three of these were on La Cura Island, and namely the Church of Sts. Serge and Bacchus, founded by the Fraudana and Calciamiri families, and the Church of St. Matthew, with a monastery annexed to each.

The first Church suggests that, in addition to the presence of ecclesiastical and trading facilities, there may even have been a permanent garrison, seeing as in areas under Byzantine sway these two Saints were venerated as patrons of the army.

The ruins of a rural building and of the Church of Sts. John and Paul may be seen in a sixteenth century drawing of La Cura, perhaps one of the few surviving records of the Island ever having been inhabited at all. Today, no trace of these constructions remains.

Since the twelfth century La Cura Island has been variously deserted or farmed, or its banks have been used as fishing grounds.

Santa Cristina

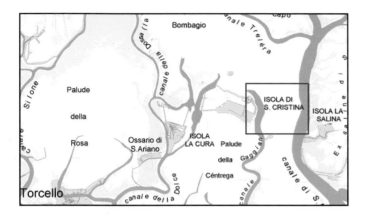

The Island was once part of an archipelago called Ammiana of which little is currently left.
The Island was colonised by former inhabitants of Altino, growing into an important centre governed by officials called "tribunes", who depended directly on Torcello.

When Jesolo and Eraclea were devastated in the eighth century, the refugees once more settled in Ammiana thus boosting the population even further.

By the seventh century Ammiana was a notable settlement with many churches and monasteries, whose construction had begun in the fourth century and was to continue unabated through to the twelfth.

An ecclesiastical establishment dedicated to St. Mark and governed by Benedictine nuns was built around the seventh century under the patronage of the Falier family. It essentially stood where the Island of St. Christine stands today.

The relics of St. Christine were smuggled out of Constantinople and secretly brought to the Monastery in

1325. Henceforth, the Church and Convent that till then had been referred to as being of St. Mark, were named after the Saint of Tyre.

Fearing the Monastery might crumple owing to the progressive erosion of the Island by water, in 1340 the nuns moved to the Convent of St. Mary of the Angels on Murano Island, only to be ordered back to the abandoned Monastery by the Senate.

By 1452 living conditions in the Monastery had become highly precarious and the only nun in residence was allowed to move to the establishment annexed to St. Anthony's Church in Torcello. After being brought to the latter Church in transit, the relics of St. Christine were finally moved to the Church of St. Francis of the Vineyard, where they are still held today. The complex at Ammiana was hence gradually evacuated owing to the progressive erosion of the Island and by the mid fifteenth century all the buildings were deserted. Despite the efforts by the Government of the Republic to counter the erosion, Ammiana was finally submerged by the encroaching waters. Only scattered strips of land persist to this day, of which St. Christine is the most consistent, but no trace of any building is to be found.

As may be seen in a map dated 1770, except for marshes where today there are shallow fishing banks, St. Christine had already attained its current appearance at the time. The map also shows that a building stood where the current one stands.

The Island is today privately owned and in an excellent state of repair. It has been raised and enclosed by embankments. Non-built up areas are given over to a vineyard and to vegetable and flower gardening. A portion of the Island has been reserved as a shallow fishing bank.

La Salina

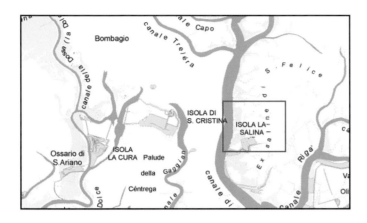

A mere "morsel" of its former self, the island is what survives of the Archipelago of Ammiana. It was first settled by a colony of refugees fleeing from Altino in the fifth century and prospered well into the ninth.

From the records it appears that a monastery with an annexed church dedicated to Sts. Felix and Fortunatus already stood in 889 in the area now occupied by the saltpans. It was in fact founded by the Benedictine monks of St. Stephen of Altino who had fled their former monastery to escape the Magyar invasion.

Thanks to its many beneficiaries and accumulated wealth, the Monastery quickly grew in status, so much so that it soon became a greatly coveted final resting place for many a Chief Magistrate of Venice, including Doge Orso Partecipazio.

From the twelfth to the fourteenth centuries a severe deterioration of the habitat led to the gradual evacuation of the Island and of the nearby Costanziaca.

The last monks to leave Sts. Felix and Fortunatus around the mid fifteenth century founded the Cloister of Sts. Philip and James in Venice.

The ecclesiastical buildings which are still recorded in a map dated 1500 soon became derelict and were demolished.

St. Felix's knoll had been deserted for centuries when in 1844 the site was chosen for the construction of management facilities for the extraction of sea salt in the adjacent greater bog.

The excavations uncovered the foundations of the ancient parish church of the High Middle Ages whose outline could still be clearly discerned. The saltpan was completed in 1857.

Salt production came to an end in 1913 and the Island was settled by several families occupied in vegetable gardening, orchard growing and fishing.

A large, possibly utility outbuilding with an open courtyard for the by-then discontinued farm appears in lands office records dated 1932.

The two constructions still extant today appear to be the surviving corner towers of the former service building.

The Island ceased being economically exploited sometime during the second half of the twentieth century.

1992 was revival year as the island and its buildings underwent repairs and renovation works for conversion to use as farmhouse accommodation (agritourism) and for sports fishing activities.

Images of the Lagoon

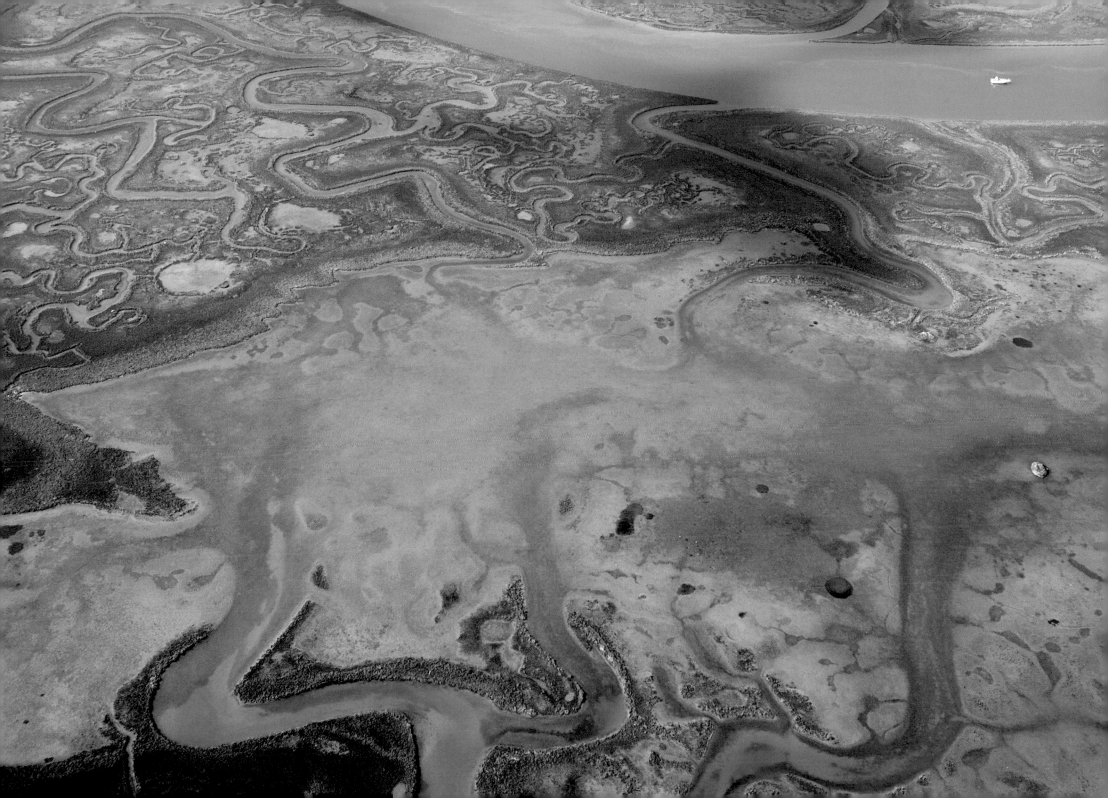

References

Chioggia
www.chioggia.org
http://217.57.31.67/sito/presentazione/index.htm

Ottagono Cà Roman
Archivio Fotografico Isole Lagunari Storia
http://194.243.104.176/website/img_laguna/info/info_isola.asp?id=36

Pellestrina
http://sbmp.provincia.venezia.it/mir/itinera/archeo/pelles0.htm
http://www.mariadinazareth.it/www2005/Apparizioni/Apparizione%20Pellestrina/Madonna%20dell'Apparizione.htm

St. Peter Octagon
Archivio Fotografico Isole Lagunari Storia
http://194.243.104.176/website/img_laguna/info/info_isola.asp?id=36

Alberoni
http://www.circologolfvenezia.it/

Fisolo
Archivio Fotografico Isole Lagunari Storia
http://194.243.104.176/website/img_laguna/info/info_isola.asp?id=31

Poveglia
Archivio Fotografico Isole Lagunari Storia
http://194.243.104.176/website/img_laguna/info/info_isola.asp?id=30

Santo Spirito
Archivio Fotografico Isole Lagunari Storia
http://194.243.104.176/website/img_laguna/info/info_isola.asp?id=28

Sacca Sessola
Archivio Fotografico Isole Lagunari Storia
http://194.243.104.176/website/img_laguna/info/info_isola.asp?id=26

Lazzaretto Vecchio
Archivio Fotografico Isole Lagunari Storia
http://194.243.104.176/website/img_laguna/info/info_isola.asp?id=27

San Clemente
Archivio Fotografico Isole Lagunari Storia
http://194.243.104.176/website/img_laguna/info/info_isola.asp?id=23

Sant'Angelo della Polvere
Archivio Fotografico Isole Lagunari Storia
http://194.243.104.176/website/img_laguna/info/info_isola.asp?id=25
http://www.provincia.venezia.it/archeove/pubblic/caselli/caselli.htm

La Grazia
Archivio Fotografico Isole Lagunari Storia
http://194.243.104.176/website/img_laguna/info/info_isola.asp?id=37

San Giorgio in Alga
Archivio Fotografico Isole Lagunari Storia
http://194.243.104.176/website/img_laguna/info/info_isola.asp?id=20

San Lazzaro degli Armeni
http://it.wikipedia.org/wiki/San_Lazzaro_degli_Armeni

Isola Campana
http://www.ik3qar.it/ita/isole/ve29/
Isola San Servolo
Archivio Fotografico Isole Lagunari Storia

http://194.243.104.176/website/img_laguna/info/info_isola.asp?id=22

Isola di S.Giorgio Maggiore
http://www.doge.it/sgiorgio/storia.htm#2
Isola della Giudecca
http://it.wikipedia.org/wiki/Isola_della_Giudecca

San Marco
http://www.basilicasanmarco.it/WAI/ita/index.bsm
http://it.wikipedia.org/wiki/Basilica_di_San_Marco_(Venezia)
http://it.wikipedia.org/wiki/Palazzo_Ducale_di_Venezia

L'Arsenale
http://it.wikipedia.org/wiki/Arsenale_di_Venezia

Porto Passeggeri
http://www.vtp.it/pages/statistiche.jsp?m=7

Fort Sant'Andrea
http://it.wikipedia.org/wiki/Forte_di_Sant'Andrea_(Venezia)

Maximilian Tower
http://www.provincia.venezia.it/archeove/pubblic/torre/torre.htm

Bacan
http://www.veniceguide.net/veneziani./htm

Lido Airport
http://www.veneziaconvention.com/aree/esterni.asp?MenuButton=0&SEZ=esterni&SEZMED=1&ARRIVO=1
Isola di San Secondo
Archivio Fotografico Isole Lagunari Storia

http://194.243.104.176/website/img_laguna/info/info_isola.asp?id=17

Liberty Bridge
http://www.provincia.venezia.it/prefettura/ponte.htm

San Michele
Archivio Fotografico Isole Lagunari Storia
http://194.243.104.176/website/img_laguna/info/info_isola.asp?id=14

Lazzaretto Nuovo
Archivio Fotografico Isole Lagunari Storia
http://194.243.104.176/website/img_laguna/info/info_isola.asp?id=16

Isola delle Trezze
Archivio Fotografico Isole Lagunari Storia
http://194.243.104.176/website/img_laguna/info/info_isola.asp?id=19

Murano
http://it.wikipedia.org/wiki/Murano

San Giacomo in Paludo
http://www.forumlagunavenezia.org/italian/
http://194.243.104.176/website/img_laguna/

San Francesco nel deserto
Archivio Fotografico Isole Lagunari Storia
http://194.243.104.176/website/img_laguna/info/info_isola.asp?id=11

Carbonera and Tessera
 Archivio Fotografico Isole Lagunari Storia
http://194.243.104.176/website/img_laguna/info/info_isola.asp?id=8
Mazzorbo

http://digilander.libero.it/venexian/ita/mazzorbo.htm
Il piano di attacco austriaco a Venezia
Marsilio

Burano
http://www.hotelcentralevenezia.it/italia/3starsinfo/burano.htm

Ex ridotto Crevan
http://www.forumlagunavenezia.org/italian/isole/crevan.html

Torcello
http://www.forumlagunavenezia.org/italian/isole/torcello.html

Ossario di Sant'Ariano
Archivio Fotografico Isole Lagunari Storia
http://194.243.104.176/website/img_laguna/info/info_isola.asp?id=4

La Cura
http://www.forumlagunavenezia.org/italian/Aindex-venezia.html

Santa Cristina
Archivio Fotografico Isole Lagunari Storia
http://194.243.104.176/website/img_laguna/info/info_isola.asp?id=2

La Salina
Archivio Fotografico Isole Lagunari Storia
http://194.243.104.176/website/img_laguna/info/info_isola.asp?id=2

Remarks